The Surnames of Derry

by
Brian Mitchell

Genealogy Centre
Derry

The Genealogy Centre gratefully acknowledges the generous financial support of Du Pont (U.K.) Ltd.

Genealogy Centre
Inner City Trust
Heritage Library
14 Bishop Street
Derry
BT48 6PW

Published in 1992

ISBN 0 9513318 1 7

Cover Design by Joe Campbell
Typesetting by Celine Byrne of Guildhall Press

Front cover: The city of Derry at night.
(Photograph: Courtesy of the Northern Ireland Tourist Board)

Acknowledgements

Thanks to Pam Carlin, Noreen Hazlett, Joe McCallion, Marguerite McDevitt, Eunan McFeeley, Mary Quigley and Danny Toland, all of the Inner City Trust, who did much good preparatory work. Thank you to my father, Samuel Mitchell, who produced the County maps.

This book would not have been possible without the commitment and professionalism of Guildhall Press: many thanks to Paul Hippsley for his advice on all aspects of publishing, and Celine Byrne, Joe McAllister and Michael McCarron for typesetting and design.

INTRODUCTION

The 1989 Foyle Community Directory lists 1,860 unique surnames in Derry City. Each of these surnames bears a distinctive history and taken as a whole they are a record of population movements into the Derry area over the past 400 years. Derry's dynamic history can be seen in the richness and variety of her surnames.

In this book an attempt has been made to explain the origins of all these surnames. To aid understanding, the surnames are classified, wherever possible, in two ways. Firstly by cultural origin and secondly by surname origin.

CULTURAL ORIGIN

Generally Derry surnames can be identified as originating from one of three distinct groupings:

1) Gaelic - either Irish or Highland Scottish.
2) English/Lowland Scottish.
3) 20th century arrivals from outside the British Isles.

SURNAME ORIGIN

Surnames, furthermore, can be divided into four classes as they are generally based on or derived from one of the following:

1) The First Name of an ancestor.
2) Local Names - whether a physical feature or an actual place name.
3) Occupational Names.
4) Nicknames - referring to a person's physical appearance, character or habits.

Some names remain unexplained as their origins are not yet understood or documented. In all, the origins of 102 surnames could not be identified in the reference books listed elsewhere in the Introduction. To fill this gap in our knowledge we contacted a bearer of each of these surnames by either letter or telephone for any information they held on the origins of their name.

The number following each surname simply refers to the number of entries in the Foyle Directory.

For easy reference the top 140 surnames in the Derry area are listed in descending order. The three commonest names have Donegal origins with Doherty heading the way with 523 entries, followed by McLaughlin on 276 and Gallagher with 170 entries. By way of contrast 808 surnames occur only once.

County maps of England and Wales, Scotland and Ireland are also included as surnames can often be identified with a particular county or number of counties.

Today surnames mean an inherited family name, originally it meant simply an additional name. In early society our ancestors had single personal names which were quite sufficient to distinguish them in small communities. As societies became more complex and officialdom was created it became essential to add a second name: in essence an early form of the National Insurance Number. These additional names or bynames were not, at first, passed on from one generation to the next. They did, however, create a stock of names which were later turned into hereditary family names.

Of great importance to the understanding of surnames in the Derry area are the differing origins and developments of surnaming systems in Irish and Highland Scottish society as compared to England and the Lowlands of Scotland.

ENGLAND

The use of bynames commenced in France about the year 1000 and they were introduced to England with the Norman Conquest from 1066. Slowly these bynames were turned into hereditary family names and by 1400 nearly all English people inherited a surname at birth.

The most noticeable characteristic of English surnames is their extraordinary number and variety. Of the 50 commonest names in England in 1856, 27 were derived from the more popular first names, 13 from occupations, 7 from localities and 3 from nicknames.

Owing to the relatively small stock of popular first names, whether of Celtic, Germanic, Scandinavian, Norman or Biblical origins, surnames based on the first name of father or other ancestor tend to be very common. By contrast surnames based on local names are very varied owing to the vast number of different local names; the biggest set of these are based on the names of English villages.

Through both the shortening of the more popular first names into pet forms and by the addition of suffixes, known as diminutives, such as cock, kin, ot, et, un, in and el the stock of surnames was greatly increased. Thus surnames such as Adcock and Hewett were created which literally meant young or little Adam and Hugh respectively. These surnames would originally have denoted either descent from, or employee of, the person named.

LOWLAND SCOTLAND

The naming tradition of Lowland Scotland and the Borders of Scotland tended to develop along English lines as it was subject to English influence. For example, many Scottish surnames from the Central Lowlands are habitation names derived from places in this region.

IRELAND

Ireland was one of the first countries to adopt a system of hereditary surnames which developed from a more ancient system of clan and sept names. From the 11th century each family began to adopt its own distinctive family name generally derived from the first name of an ancestor who lived in or about the 10th century.

The surname was formed by prefixing either Mac (Son of) or O (Grandson or descendant of) to the ancestor's name. Surnames in Ireland, therefore, tended to identify membership of a "sept". A sept can be identified as "a group of persons who, or whose immediate and known ancestors, bore a common surname and inhabited the same locality". As a consequence Gaelic-Irish surnames are still very dominant and numerous in the very districts where their names originated.

HIGHLAND SCOTLAND

In the Highlands of Scotland surnames were also of Gaelic origin and were typically formed by prefixing Mac (Son of) to an ancestor's name.

The Highlands were organised in a "clan" system. As clan is an anglicised form of the Gaelic word for children it implies that every member of the clan descends from the tribal father from whom the clan derives its name. Be careful though in assuming that Scottish clan membership denotes common origins; it does not necessarily do so.

In Ireland it is generally accepted that members of an Irish sept have a common tribal ancestor. In Scotland a number of families, having different surnames, comprised a clan which was known by the name of the leading sept in it. Furthermore the advisability of belonging to a large and powerful clan resulted in the assumption of the clan surname by persons who merely lived in its territory and were of no kindred to the chief.

WALES

In Wales the stock of surnames is not large as they were, for the most part, formed from the forename of the father in the genitive case, thus John's son became Jones and Evan's son became Evans.

Although Gaelic society was one of the first to adopt a system of hereditary surnames it was also one of the last to perpetuate fixed surnames. People in these societies, in the early 18th century, were often designated by their genealogies stretching back five or more generations. For example Shane O'Neill of Shane's Castle, County Antrim, styled himself on the family vault, which he built in 1722, as "Shane McBrien McPhelim McShane McBrien McPhelim O'Neill Esq". Here is family history in one name stretching back over 200 years. The last-named Phelim was Felim "The Lame" who was Prince of Clanaboy from 1529 to 1533.

Owing to its history all the above naming traditions are well represented in Derry; from the numerical strength of a small number of surnames of Gaelic-Irish origin to the great richness and variety of surnames of English and Scottish origin, where Norman-French influence held sway.

In the 12th century the Normans were the first to bring English-style surnames to Ireland. It was a series of immigrations, however, during the 17th century, coming from the Lowlands and Borders of Scotland and, to a lesser extent, from various parts of England which established a great variety of new surnames alongside the existing Gaelic-Irish ones in the Derry area.

Substantial numbers of Scottish families entered Ulster through Derry and settled in the Foyle Valley. Pacification of the riding families of the Borders (who lived by cattle stealing and kidnapping) which began in earnest from 1603 with the Union of the Crowns of England and Scotland; religious conflict in South-West Scotland in the late 1670s which culminated in the severe persecution of Presbyterians, in the so-called "Killing Times", in Ayrshire in the period 1684-1688; and four successive harvest failures, in the 1690s, throughout both the Highlands and the Lowlands, all generated successive waves of Scottish emigrants to Ulster.

English settlers, mostly drawn from the northern counties of Cheshire, Cumberland, Lancashire, Northumberland, Yorkshire and Westmorland tended to favour settlement along the Lagan Valley in the east of the Province.

The London Companies who planted much of County Derry found it hard to hold their ill-prepared and ill-suited English settlers. The Companies, therefore, looked to the durable Scottish farmers to tenant their estates. As a consequence surnames of Scottish origin dominate the Plantation names of the Derry area and owing to the Highland influence many of these names have Gaelic origins.

ANGLICISATION

From the 17th century Gaelic surnames were anglicised. Some names were translated into English while others were changed to a similar-sounding English name. This process of anglicisation, together with illiteracy, gave rise to numerous spelling variations of the same name. Uniformity in spelling surnames is really a phenomenon of the 20th century. The clergy, in entering relevant details on say a baptism register, often had to write down names based on pronunciation as many people could not write down or spell their name. Names of Gaelic origin were, furthermore, disguised by the widespread discarding of the prefixes of Mac, Mc and O in the 18th century.

Anglicisation will, in many cases, obscure the true origin of a surname. For example Smith many be an English name or the anglicisation of the Gaelic McGowan (Son of Smith). Many surnames in the Derry area, such as Clarke, Green, Johnson, Mitchell and Rodgers, could have originated independently in England, Scotland or Ireland; only detailed family history research will confirm the actual origin.

20th CENTURY SETTLERS

More recent arrivals from outside the British Isles have also contributed a small but interesting collection of surnames in the Derry area.

An Italian community with surnames such as Battisti, Yanerelli and Fiorentini settled in Derry in the 1920s. They tended to set up in either the restaurant or ice cream trade.

A Jewish community with names such as Schenkel, Szilagyi, Spain and Watchman settled in Derry and worshipped in a synagogue in Kennedy Place.

A thriving Indian community has been established in the city since the 1950s, most of whom originate from the Punjab in Northern India.

United States Navy personnel stationed in the one-time Communications Base have married local girls and made their roots here.

More recent immigrants to the area are the Chinese with origins in Hong Kong's rural villages.

Standard reference books were used to compile this dictionary. They include:

Irish Families by Edward MacLysaght.
The Surnames of Ireland by Edward MacLysaght.
The Book of Ulster Surnames by Robert Bell.
A Dictionary of British Surnames by P.H. Reaney.
A Dictionary of Surnames by Patrick Hanks and Flavia Hodges.
The Penguin Dictionary of Surnames by Basil Cottle.
The Concise Oxford Dictionary of English Place-Names by Eilert Ekwall.
The Surnames of Scotland by George F. Black.
The Clans and Tartans of Scotland by Robert Bain.
Welsh Surnames by T.J. Morgan and Prys Morgan.

These reference books should be consulted by those who wish to delve deeper into the subject of surname origins.

THE TOP 140 SURNAMES IN DERRY
Source: Foyle Community Directory

SURNAME	NUMBER	SURNAME	NUMBER
Doherty	523	Simpson	49
McLaughlin	246	Stewart	49
Gallagher	170	McCauley	48
Kelly	142	Walker	47
Moore	125	Curran	46
Coyle	116	Taylor	46
Harkin	114	Johnston	45
Bradley	110	Murray	44
Campbell	110	Donnelly	43
McDaid	105	Duddy	42
Lynch	96	Gillespie	41
Brown	91	Moran	41
O'Donnell	91	Logue	40
Hamilton	89	Ward	40
Smith	84	McGilloway	39
Hegarty	72	Breslin	38
Quigley	69	McGinley	38
Duffy	68	Porter	38
Barr	65	McIntyre	37
Thompson	65	Martin	37
McCallion	64	McBride	36
Carlin	63	McKinney	36
McCloskey	60	Murphy	36
Wilson	60	O'Hagan	36
McDermott	59	Ferguson	35
Boyle	58	McMonagle	35
Morrison	58	Keys	34
O'Kane	55	Orr	34
Cassidy	53	Sweeney	34
McGowan	53	Clarke	33
McCafferty	52	McFadden	33
Mullan	51	Young	32
Devine	50	Canning	31
O'Neill	50	Colhoun	31

Armstrong	30
Craig	30
McCarron	30
White	30
Harrigan	29
Downey	28
McMenamin	28
Miller	28
Cunningham	27
McClelland	27
McGuinness	27
Peoples	27
Toland	27
Burke	26
Friel	26
Grant	26
Jackson	26
Long	26
McCay	26
McClay	26
Black	25
Boyd	25
Burns	25
Deery	25
Doran	25
Lyttle	25
Magee	25
McColgan	25
McKeever	25
Browne	24
Donaghy	24
Kerr	24
McCool	24
McCorkell	24
McCormick	24
O'Reilly	24
Wylie	24
Allen	23
Fleming	23
Hasson	23
Millar	23
Nichol	23
Tracey	23
Walsh	23
Anderson	22
Bell	22
Bonner	22
Casey	22
Devlin	22
Gormley	22
Hutton	22
McCourt	22
McDowell	22
McElhinney	22
O'Connor	22
Wallace	22
Crossan	21
Glen	21
Green	21
Heaney	21
Henderson	21
McCartney	21
McConnell	21
McIvor	21
Watson	21
Begley	20
Ferry	20
Keenan	20
McClintock	20
McCready	20
Mooney	20
Norris	20

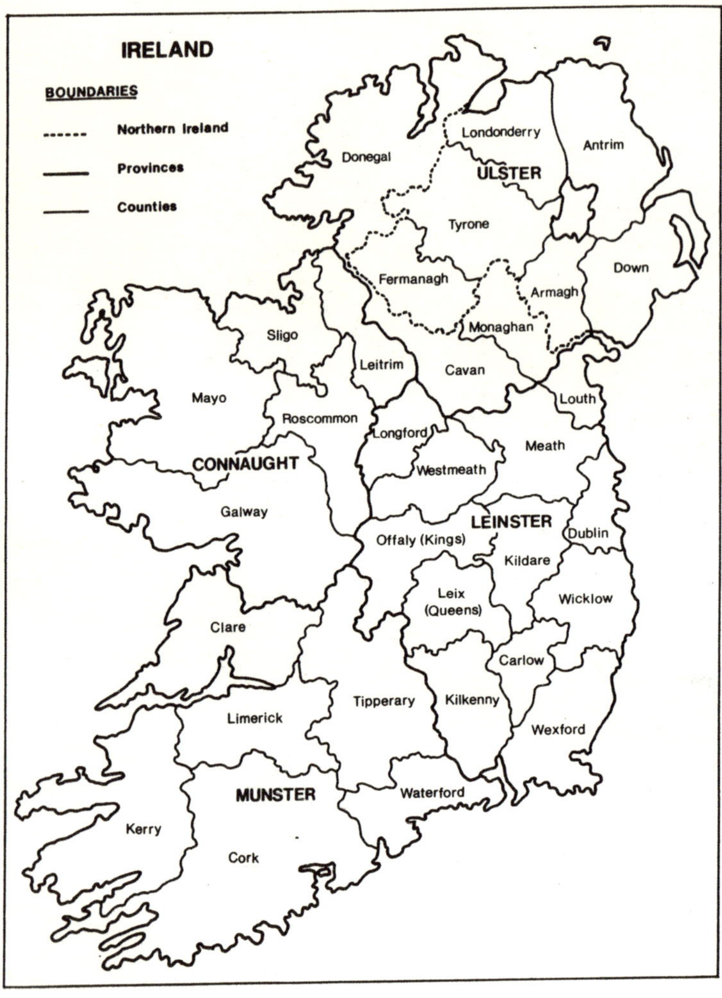
IRELAND
BOUNDARIES
Northern Ireland
Provinces
Counties
Donegal
Londonderry
Antrim
ULSTER
Tyrone
Fermanagh
Armagh
Down
Monaghan
Sligo
Leitrim
Cavan
Mayo
Roscommon
Louth
Longford
Meath
CONNAUGHT
Westmeath
Galway
LEINSTER
Offaly (Kings)
Dublin
Kildare
Leix
(Queens)
Wicklow
Clare
Carlow
Tipperary
Kilkenny
Limerick
Wexford
MUNSTER
Waterford
Kerry
Cork

SCOTLAND
COUNTIES BEFORE 1975
Orkney Islands
Shetland Islands
Caithness
Sutherland
OUTER
HEBRIDES
Lewis
N. Uist
S. Uist
Skye
INNER
HEBRIDES
Ross and Cromarty
Nairn
Moray
Banff
Aberdeen
Inverness
Kincardine
Angus
Perth
Mull
Argyll
Clackmannan
Fife
Kinross
Jura
Islay
Dunbarton
Stirling
West Lothian
East Lothian
Midlothian
Renfrew
Lanark
Berwick
Bute
Peebles
Selkirk
Roxburgh
Arran
Ayr
Dumfries
Kirkcudbright
Wigtown
IRELAND
ENGLAND

ENGLAND AND WALES
COUNTIES BEFORE 1975
SCOTLAND
IRELAND
Northumberland
Cumberland
Durham
Westmorland
Isle of Man
Yorkshire
Lancashire
Anglesey
Flint
Cheshire
Derby
Nottingham
Lincoln
Caernarvon
Denbigh
Merioneth
Stafford
Rutland
Norfolk
Montgomery
Shropshire
Leicester
Huntington
Cambridge
Warwick
Northampton
Suffolk
Cardigan
Radnor
Worcester
Bedford
Brecknock
Hereford
Pembroke
Carmarthen
Oxford
Buckingham
Hertford
Essex
Gloucester
Monmouth
Glamorgan
Greater London
Berkshire
Wiltshire
Surrey
Kent
Somerset
Hampshire
Sussex
Devon
Dorset
Isle of Wight
Cornwall

A

Abel (2) *English* and *Scottish.* Derived from the biblical name which was a popular first name in the Middle Ages. It was recorded in Scotland from the 13th century.

Abraham (1) *English* and *Scottish.* Derived from the old testament patriarch whose name meant father of a multitude of nations. It was recorded as a surname in Scotland from the 12th century.

Acheson (3) This is the *Scottish* spelling of Atkinson (See Atkinson). As Lords Gosford the Achesons of Edinburgh founded the linen town of Lurgan in the 17th century.

Adair (15) *Scottish.* Derived from the Old English personal name of Edgar. The name was first recorded in the province of Galloway in the 13th century and by the 14th century the Edgars of Dumfriesshire were being recorded as Adair.

Adams (11) Can be of *English, Scottish* or *Irish* origin. In England and Scotland it was derived from the popular medieval christian name of Adam. In the Highlands of Scotland the Adams were a sept of Clan Gordon while in Ireland a number of distinct septs with origins in Counties Armagh, Cavan and Monaghan anglicised their name to Adams.

Adcock (2) *English.* Meaning little Adam this surname was first recorded in Leicester in the early 13th century.

Addison (1) *English* and *Scottish.* Meaning Son of Addy this name was derived from the biblical name of Adam which was recorded in the Domesday Book in 1086. This surname was most common in the eastern counties of Scotland where it first appeared in the 14th century.

Agnew (1) Can be of *English, Scottish* or *Irish* origin. Derived from Agneaux in Normandy a family of this name accompanied William the Conqueror to England in 1066. One branch came to Ulster with John de Courcy's army in the 12th century. Another branch settled in Wigtownshire, Scotland and descendants of these came to Ulster in the 17th century. In Ulster a sept of hereditary poets to the

Clandeboy O'Neills acquired the surname Agnew.

Aherne (1) *Irish.* This sept originated in East Clare but later settled in County Cork.

Ahmed (1) There are 11 listings of this name in the telephone directories of Eire. In Northern Ireland there are 4 occurrences of the name; one each in Ballymena, Derry, Dungannon and Lurgan.

Aiken (7) *Scottish.* Meaning little Adam Aiken became a common surname in Ayrshire. *Irish.* Some of the County Tyrone sept of O'Hagan (See O'Hagan) may have anglicised their name to Aiken.

Akroyd (1) *English.* Derived from a local name referring to a dweller by a clearing in an oak forest. The name was most common in West Yorkshire from the 17th century.

Alexander (2) *Scottish.* Introduced from England this christian name became a popular surname on the west coast, particularly in Kintyre and Ayrshire. There were Alexander septs belonging to Clans MacAlister, Donald, MacArthur and MacDonnell.

Alford (2) *English* and *Scottish.* Derived from place names recorded in the Domesday Book of 1086; one of which was in Surrey, the other in Lincolnshire. In Scotland it was derived from the village of Alford in Aberdeenshire.

Algeo (1) *English* and *Scottish.* A variant of the Old English first name Elgar. In the 16th century several families of this name, of Italian origin, settled in Renfrewshire, Scotland.

Allan (1) *English.* Derived from the popular Norman name Alan. *Scots Gaelic.* There were several distinct septs of Allans but most stem from Clans MacFarlane and MacDonald.

Allen (23) (See Allan).

Allison (1) *English* and *Scottish.* Meaning son of Alice this surname was common in both countries from the 13th to the 17th century. In Scotland the Allisons were also an offshoot of Clan MacAlister.

Anderson (22) *Scottish.* Meaning son of Andrew this name can be found throughout Scotland. The Andersons were a sept of Clan Donald on Islay and Kintyre and of Clan Chattan in Northeast Scotland as well as being one of the smaller riding clans of the Scottish Borders.

Andrews (6) This *Lowland Scottish* name means son of Andrew. (See Anderson)

Ansell (2) *English.* Derived from an Old German personal name meaning god-helmet.

Answell (1) A variant of Ansell. (See Ansell)

Anthony (2) *English* and *Scottish.* Derived from a Latin personal name which was popular throughout Europe. It was recorded in both countries from the 13th century.

Appleby (1) *English* and *Scottish.* Derived from place names found in Leicestershire, Lincolnshire and Westmorland which meant Apple Farm. It was recorded in Scotland from the 13th century.

Aquino (1) The bearer of this name came to Derry with the U.S. Navy in 1960 and settled here. Although originally *Spanish* in origin the family came to the United States from the Philippines where the grandfather had emigrated to.

Arbuckle (15) *Scottish.* Derived from a place name in Lanarkshire, meaning height of the shepherd.

Archibald (2) *English* and *Scottish.* Derived from a Norman given name which was recorded in the Domesday Book of 1086. Recorded as a surname in Scotland from the 12th century, the name became especially common around Edinburgh. In some cases Gillespie was anglicised to Archibald. (See Gillespie)

Armstrong (30) *Scottish.* Acquiring lands in the Scottish Borders in the 14th century the Armstrongs became one of the most powerful of the riding clans. At the height of their power they could muster an army of 3,000 men. In the 16th century neither the English or the Scottish crowns could control their forays for cattle and loot.

Arnold (1) *English* and *Scottish.* Derived either from a Norman personal name, meaning eagle-power, or from place names, meaing eagle-nook, found in Nottinghamshire and East Yorkshire. It was first recorded in Scotland from the 12th century.

Arnott (1) *Scottish.* Derived from the lands of Arnot in Kinross-shire. It may also be a variant of Arnold. (See Arnold)

Arthur (9) *English* and *Scottish.* Derived from the Celtic personal name which the tales of King Arthur and his Round Table popularised. A Norman family of the name settled in Limerick in the 12th century. It may also be a variant of the Scottish McArthur. (SeeMcArthur)

Ashenhurst (1) *English.* Derived from a local name for someone who lived by a hill on which ash trees grew. A variant of the name, Ashurst is found chiefly in Lancashire.

Ashford (3) *English.* Derived from various place names found in Devon, Derbyshire, Essex, Shropshire and Surrey, meaning ash-tree ford.

Askin (1) *English.* Derived from an Old Norse personal name meaning god-kettle. It probably refers to the sacrificial cauldron used in pagan ceremonies.

Aspel (1) This is a recorded variant of Archibald. (See Archibald)

Assarpour (1) In all of Ireland the only reference to Assarpour in the telephone directories is in Derry.

Atalli (1) Originating from the town of Mosul in Northern Iraq this name came to Derry in the mid-1970s.

Atcheson (3) (See Acheson)

Atkinson (2) *English.* Meaning son of little Adam Atkinson became particularly common in the North of England. With the 17th century plantation many families of the name settled in Counties Armagh and Fermanagh.

Atwal (1) *English.* A variant of Attwell which was derived from a local name for someone who lived by a spring or stream.

Austin (10) *English* and *Scottish.* Derived from the personal name Augustine, meaning venerable. It was first recorded in Ireland in the 14th century.

Avery (1) Can be of *English, Scottish* or *Irish* origin. In England and Scotland it derived from the Germanic personal name Aubrey. In Ireland it may be a shortened form of the County Down sept of McAvery.

Ayling (1) *English.* Derived from an Anglo-Saxon byname, meaning prince.

Ayton (2) *Scottish.* Derived from the lands of Ayton in Berwickshire, meaning town on the River Eye.

B

Baber (2) *English.* A Somerset name of uncertain origin.

Badham (1) *English.* Derived from the West Midlands place name, meaning Beada's homestead. *Welsh.* Derived from Abadam which means son of Adam. In Wales ab or ap before the christian name had the same effect as s or son after the name in England.

Bailey (1) *English* and *Scottish.* Derived from the occupational name for a bailiff. Lanarkshire, West Lothian and Inverness-shire in Scotland will be the homeland of the majority of Ulster Baileys.

Baird (7) *Scottish.* Derived from the gaelic word for a bard or poet Clan Baird were granted lands in Lanarkshire in the early 14th century by Robert the Bruce. From there they later spread to Banffshire and Aberdeenshire.

Baker (7) *English.* This occupational name referring to someone who baked bread was first recorded in Ireland in the 13th century.

Baldrick (8) *English.* Derived from a Germanic personal name meaning bold ruler. This surname was particularly associated with East Anglia. In the mid-17th century Baldricks settled in North Donegal.

Balentine (1) (See Ballantine)

Ball (12) *English* and *Scottish.* This name has various origins including: a nickname for a short, overweight person; a local name for someone who lived by a rounded hill; and an Old Norse personal name. It was introduced into Ireland from the 12th century.

Ballantine (2) *Scottish.* Derived from the lands of Ballenden in the Borders, meaning farmstead of the dean.

Ballard (2) *English* and *Scottish.* Derived from a nickname referring to a bald-headed man it is a common surname in Worcestershire. It was introduced into Ireland by the Normans in the 12th century.

Balmer (1) *English* and *Scottish.* This occupational name referred to a person who was a seller of perfumes and spices.

Bamford (1) *English.* Derived from various place names meaning a ford which could be crossed by means of a footbridge. The two main places of this name were in Derbyshire and Lancashire.

Bannon (2) *Irish.* Septs of this name originated in Counties Fermanagh and Offaly.

Barber (6) *English* and *Scottish.* This occupational name referred in the Middle Ages to someone who cut hair, shaved beards, pulled teeth and practised surgery. It was recorded in Ireland from the 13th century.

Barkley (1) *Scottish.* Derived from a number of English place names, meaning birch wood this clan traces its descent from a Norman, Walter de Berkeley, the Chamberlain of Scotland in 1165. The clan acquired lands in Kincardineshire.

Barnett (4) *English* and *Scottish.* Derived either from the personal name Bernard or from various place names signifying a locality cleared by burning.

Barr (65) *Scottish.* Derived from various place names in South-West Scotland, meaning height or hill. *English.* The name has various origins including: a local name for someone who lived by a gateway or barrier; an occupational name for a maker of bars; and a nickname for a tall, thin person.

Barras (1) May be variants of Barr (See Barr) or Barrow (See Barrow). Barros of Spanish origin refers to someone who lived on muddy land.

Barratt (1) (See Barrett)

Barren (1) (See Barron)

Barrett (14) *English.* This name has various origins including: a variant of the personal name Bernard; a nickname for a quarrelsome person; and an occupational name for a cap maker. The surname came to Ireland with the Normans.

Barron (4) Can be of *English, Scottish* or *Irish* origin. In England it derived as a nickname for someone who was proud or haughty. In Scotland baron was the term used for small land owners in gaelic society while in Ireland, as McBarron, they were a branch of the O'Neills in County Armagh.

Barrow (2) *English.* Derived from various local place names referring to a dweller by a grave or to someone who lived by a hill or burial mound.

Bartlett (1) *English* and *Scottish.* Meaning little Bartholomew this medieval personal name originally referred to someone who was rich in land. The surname is common in Dorset, Somerset and Oxfordshire.

Barton (1) *English* and *Scottish.* Derived from a number of place names meaning barley-farm. It was recorded in Ireland from the 13th century.

Barwise (1) *English.* Derived from a place name in Westmorland meaning hills.

Bastow (1) *English.* Derived from the West Yorkshire place name of Bairstow, meaning berry-place.

Bates (2) *English* and *Scottish.* Meaning son of Bartholomew (See Bartlett) this surname was recorded in Ireland from the mid-17th century.

Baumann (1) *German.* A variant of Bauer which meant either peasant or neighbour. At a later date this surname was adopted by the Jewish community.

Baxendale (1) *English.* Derived from the Lancashire place name of Baxenden, meaning bakestone valley. A bakestone was a flat stone on which bread was baked.

Baxter (1) *Scottish.* Derived from the occupational name for a baker. It is possible that the first Baxters were the bakers at the royal palace at Forfar in Angus. The Baxters were also a sept of Clan MacMillan.

Beadsworth (1) *English.* Perhaps derived from the Lancashire place name of Beardsworth or the Warwickshire place name of Bedworth.

Beagan (1) *Irish.* This sept originated in County Kildare but a branch later migrated to Kerry.

Beaton (1) *English* and *Scottish.* Derived either from the personal name Beatrice or from the French place name of Bethune. In the 16th and 17th centuries the Beatons were hereditary physicians on the Isle of Skye.

Beattie (10) *Scottish.* Derived from the personal name Bate, which was in turn derived from Bartholomew (See Bartlett). The Beatties became well known in Galloway and the Borders of Scotland, where they were one of the smaller riding clans.

Beedham (1) The bearer of this name came to Derry from Cambridgeshire, England. It is a variant of Badham (See Badham).

Beehan (1) A variant of Beagan. (See Beagan)

Beggs (1) Can be of *English*, *Scottish* or *Irish* origin. In England and Lowland Scotland Beggs derived from a nickname meaning large or strong while in Ireland and Highland Scotland it derived from the gaelic for little or small.

Begley (20) *Irish*. A County Donegal sept, a branch of which migrated to County Kerry in the 15th century as mercenary soldiers, known as galloglasses.

Beirne (2) *Irish*. Derived from the Norse forename Bjorn this sept originated in Counties Mayo and Roscommon.

Bell (22) *English* and *Scottish*. Bell variously derived from an occupational name for a bell ringer, from a nickname meaning beautiful or from a local name for someone who lived near a bell. It was a common name in the Scottish Borders where they were one of the riding clans. Bell was also common in the Isles where they were a branch of Clan MacMillan.

Benham (1) *English*. Derived from villages of that name in Berkshire, meaning Benna's river-meadow. *Scottish*. Derived from the lands of Benholm in Angus. The family granted these lands adopted it as their surname in the 13th century.

Bennett (2) *English* and *Scottish*. Derived from the christian name Benet which in turn was derived from Benedict, a common christian name from the 12th century onwards. It was recorded as a surname in Scotland from the 15th century. Bennett was introduced to Ireland in the 14th century by an Anglo-Norman family.

Benzie (1) *Scottish*. Meaning little Benedict (See Bennett) this surname was first recorded at Inverurie in Aberdeenshire in the 15th century.

Beresford-Ash (1) *English*. A double-barrelled name. Beresford is derived from the Staffordshire place name, meaning beaver ford while Ash is derived from a local name for someone who lived near an ash tree.

Bergin (1) *Irish*. This sept originated in County Offaly but settled in County Leix.

Berthold (1) *German.* Derived from the personal name Bertwald, meaning bright-rule.

Best (5) *English* and *Scottish.* Meaning beast this name originated either as a nickname for a brutal person or as an occupational name for someone who looked after cattle. It was first recorded in Scotland at Edinburgh in the 15th century.

Bicknell (1) *English.* Derived from the Somerset place name of Bickenhall, meaning Bicca's hall.

Biddle (2) *English.* A variant of Beadle which was an occupational name for a medieval official who acted as an usher in a court of justice. At a later date a beadle was the village constable.

Bigger (1) *Scottish.* Derived from the lands of Biggar in Lanarkshire. The family granted these lands adopted it as their surname in the 12th century.

Birney (5) A variant of McBurney. (See McBurney)

Birt (1) *English.* A variant of Burt which derived from the Germanic personal name Berht. It has been established in Derry since the early 18th century.

Bishop (1) *Irish* and *Scots Gaelic.* Derived from the anglicisation of a name which, when translated, meant son of the servant of the Bishop (See Gillespie). *English.* Derived either as an occupational name for someone who worked in the house of the Bishop or as a nickname for a person with the bearing of a Bishop.

Black (25) *English.* Derived from a nickname which can mean both 'black' or 'dark' and 'white' or 'pale' depending on the original language root. *Scots Gaelic.* Septs of this name belonged to Clans Gregor, Lamont and MacLean. Many members of Clan Gregor and Clan Lamont adopted this colour name on their proscription by the Crown in the 17th century. Most Ulster Blacks are of this origin.

Blackburn (2) *English* and *Scottish.* Derived from various place names meaning dark stream, it is mainly found in Northern England. Blackburn was first recorded in Scotland in the 13th century and in Ireland in the 14th century.

Blackwell (1) *English.* Derived from various place names in the North and Midlands of England meaning dark spring. This surname was introduced to Ireland with the Cromwellian soldier-adventurers of the mid-17th century.

Blackwood (4) *English* and *Scottish.* Derived from various place names found in Yorkshire, Dumfriesshire and Lanarkshire, meaning dark wood.

Blain (1) *Scots Gaelic.* This abbreviated form of McBlain was associated with Ayrshire and Wigtownshire.

Blair (7) *Scottish.* Derived from various place names meaning plain, field or battlefield. As a surname Blair was frequently recorded in Scotland from the 13th century.

Blakely (3) *English* and *Scottish.* Derived from the place name of Blackley in Lancashire, meaning black wood or clearing. It was first recorded in Scotland in the 14th century where the name is particularly associated with Dumfriesshire. It first appeared in Ireland in the 17th century.

Blaney (2) *Welsh.* Derived from a local name for uplands which referred to the upper end of a valley. A family of this name settled in County Monaghan at the end of the 16th century.

Blanking (2) *English.* Perhaps derived from the place name of Blankney in Lincolnshire, meaning Blanca's island or from the nickname 'Blank' which was used to denote a man with fair hair or pale complexion.

Bleackley (1) (See Blakely)

Bleakley (1) (See Blakely)

Blee (2) This variant of Bligh can either be of *English* or *Irish* origin. In England it derived as a nickname for a cheerful person while in Ireland a Connaught sept took this name from an Old Norse personal name.

Bliss (1) *English.* Derived either from a nickname meaning cheerful or from the village of Blay in Normandy.

Boal (1) A variant of Boyle. (See Boyle)

Boardman (1) *English.* Derived from local names referring either to someone who lived in a plank-built cottage or at the edge of a village. This surname was chiefly found in Lancashire.

Boddington (1) *English.* Derived from place names located in Gloucestershire and Northamptonshire, meaning Bota's settlement and Bota's hill respectively.

Boggs (3) *English* and *Scottish.* In England Boggs is derived from a nickname meaning haughty while in Scotland it derived from a place name in Midlothian.

Bogle (4) *Scottish.* Derived from the place name of Bowgyhill in Lanarkshire. The surname was recorded in Glasgow in the late 15th century.

Boland (2) *English.* Derived from various place names meaning bow-land. *Irish.* Two septs of this name, derived from an Old Norse personal name, originated in Counties Sligo and Clare.

Bolster (2) *English.* Originating in Germany as an occupational name for a maker or seller of cushions this surname was recorded in County Cork from the early 18th century.

Bolton (3) *English* and *Scottish.* Derived from a great number of place names in Northern England, especially in Lancashire, meaning dwelling-settlement. It was first recorded in Scotland in the 13th century where it derived from an East Lothian place name. Bolton has been recorded in Ireland since medieval times.

Bond (5) *English.* Derived from the Norman term for a peasant farmer this surname has been recorded in Ireland since the early 14th century.

Bonner (22) *Irish.* This County Donegal sept, especially prominent around Ballybofey, bears one of the oldest surnames in Ireland which was first recorded in 1095. In Derry, Bonners will largely be of this origin. This surname, however, also originated in England where it derived from a nickname meaning gentle or courteous. A few settlers may have brought this name to Ulster.

Booth (1) *Northern English* and *Scottish.* Derived from a word of Scandinavan origin to denote someone who lived in a small hut, usually a temporary shelter such as a shepherd's bothy. It was recorded in Ireland from the mid-17th century.

Boreland (2) (See Borland)

Borland (2) *Scottish.* Derived from various place names meaning table land, i.e. land which supplied the landlord's table. The surname was first recorded in Ayrshire in the early 16th century.

Borrow (1) A variant of Burrow. See Burrow.

Boucher (2) A variant of Butcher. See Butcher.

Bovaird (3) *French.* Derived from the occupational name for a herdsman this name was particularly associated with County Donegal.

Bowe (1) *English.* Derived either from the occupational name for a maker or seller of bows or from a local name for someone who lived near a bridge. *Irish.* This sept which originated in County Cork also anglicised its name to Bogue, Bowes and Bowie.

Bowen (1) *Welsh.* Derived from the popular Welsh name Owain this surname meant son of Owen. (See Badham). In Ireland the County Cork sept of Bohane was sometimes anglicised to Bowen.

Bowstead (1) *English.* Probably derived from a place name meaning site of the arched bridge.

Boyce (4) *Irish.* A County Donegal sept whose name meant victorious. In Derry Boyce will largely be of this origin. *English* and *Scottish.* Derived from a local name for someone who lived near a wood. Boyce was introduced to Ireland with the Anglo-Normans in the 13th century.

Boyd (25) *Scots Gaelic.* Derived either from the place name, the Isle of Bute or from a nickname meaning 'yellow'. As well as becoming well established in Edinburgh and Ayrshire the Boyds were a sept of Clan Stewart.

Boylan (1) *Irish.* A County Monaghan sept, with origins in the Clones area, whose chief was King of Fermanagh in the 11th century. Their power was subsequently reduced and by the 14th century they were sub-lords to the McMahons.

Boyle (58) *Irish.* A County Donegal sept, with their heartland at Cloghaneely, who alongside the O'Dohertys and the O'Donnells controlled Northwest Donegal in medieval times. *English* and *Scottish.* Derived from Beauville in France a family of this name accompanied William the Conqueror to England in 1066. A branch also settled in Scotland, becoming well established in Ayrshire. The Boyles of Limavady who settled there in 1660 are of this stock.

Brace (3) *English.* Derived from occupational names for either a maker of armour or a maker of breeches.

Bracken (1) *Irish.* This sept originated on the Kildare-Offaly border.

Bradley (110) *Irish.* The territory of this sept was on the borders of Counties Derry, Donegal and Tyrone. In Derry Bradley will largely be of this origin. *Scots Gaelic*. A branch of the Irish Bradleys settled in the Western Highlands where one of its members became Abbot of Iona in the 12th century. *Lowland Scottish*. Derived from the place name of Braidlie in Roxburghshire.

Bradshaw (3) *English*. Derived from various place names meaning broad thicket, this surname was most frequent in Lancashire. Bradshaw was well established in Ireland by the early 17th century.

Brady (18) *Irish*. This powerful sept at one time ruled a large territory to the east of Cavan town in the ancient Kingdom of Breffny.

Braiden (1) *Irish*. Derived from a personal name meaning salmon this surname is mainly found in Donegal, Fermanagh and Tyrone.

Braithwaite (1) *English*. Derived from place names in Cumberland and Yorkshire, meaning broad clearing.

Branagan (2) *Irish*. This sept can trace its lineage to Eoghan, son of the 5th century Niall of the Nine Hostages. Their homeland was the ancient Kingdom of Oriel which straddled Counties Armagh and Monaghan.

Brand (1) *English* and *Scottish*. Derived from an Old English personal name meaning sword. It was first recorded in Scotland in Ayrshire in the early 14th century.

Brandon (3) *English*. Derived from various place names meaning gorse hill. In County Kerry a branch of the Fitzmaurices anglicised their name to Brandon.

Brannen (2) A variant of Brennan. See Brennan.

Branter (2) Perhaps a variant of the Scottish name Brander which was derived from the occupational name for a man who branded fish barrells.

Brattin (1) See Bratton.

Bratton (2) *English*. Derived from various place names meaning either newly cultivated settlement or settlement by the brook. The surname first appeared in Scotland in the 16th century.

Bray (4) Can be of *English*, *Scottish* or *Irish* origin. In England it derived from place names in Berkshire and Devon, meaning marsh and hill respectively. In Scotland it may be derived from one of many places called Brae while in Ireland a County Tipperary sept anglicised their name to Bray.

Bredin (6) See Braiden.

Breen (2) *Irish.* The County Donegal sept of O'Breen, who were based in Clonleigh Parish, and the County Fermanagh sept of McBreen, who trace their descent from the McMahons, had their names shortened to Breen.

Brehaut (1) In all of Ireland the only reference to Brehaut in the telephone directories is in Derry.

Brennan (10) *Irish.* Several septs of the name originated in Counties Galway, Kerry, Roscommon and Westmeath but most in Ulster will be descended from a County Fermanagh sept who trace their descent from Eoghan, son of the 5th century Niall of the Nine Hostages.

Brent (1) *English.* This surname has various origins which include; a local name for someone who lived by land which had been cleared by burning; place names in Devon and Somerset meaning steep; and a nickname for 'a criminal who had been branded'.

Bresland (5) A variant of Breslin. See Breslin.

Breslin (38) *Irish.* This Donegal sept ruled territory centred on Inniskeel on the Fanad peninsula. They later migrated to Fermanagh where they became hereditary lawyers to the Maguires.

Brett (1) *English.* Derived as a term for a Breton. The Bretons were Celts who settled in Northwest France from Southwest England in the 6th century A.D. Some of them returned to England in 1066 with the army of William the Conqueror. In Scotland the term was applied to the Celts of Strathclyde until well into the 13th century.

Brewster (1) *English* and *Scottish.* Derived from the occupational name for a brewer of ale. Originally the name only referred to female brewers but by the early 13th century the surname was being widely used in Scotland by men.

Brick (1) *Scottish.* Derived as a variant of Brigg which is the Scot's form of Bridge (See Bridge). *Irish.* A sept originating in County Waterford anglicised its name to Brick. This name is now seldom found outside Kerry.

Bridge (3) *English.* Derived as a local name for someone who lived near a bridge. In some cases it may have been an occupational name for a bridgekeeper.

Brien (1) See Breen and O'Brien.

Brinkley (1) *English.* Derived from a place name in Cambridgeshire, meaning Brynca's clearing.

Britton (2) Another form of Brett. See Brett.

Brizzel (1) Although only recorded in Northern Ireland it is a common name here with 11 listings of it in the telephone directory. The name is especially associated with the Garvagh, Kilrea, Ballymena area. Family tradition claims the name came to Ireland from France during the French Revolution of 1789.

Broderick (2) *Irish.* Two septs, originating in Counties Cork and Galway, anglicised their names to Broderick. Broderick was also a Welsh name, meaning son of Roderick.

Brolly (10) *Irish.* Derived from an Old Irish personal name and originating in County Derry this sept also had its name anglicised to Brawley.

Brothers (4) *Irish.* This form of Broderick originated in County Donegal. See Broderick. *English.* Derived from a byname meaning younger son of.

Brotherton (1) *Scottish.* Derived from the place name of Brothstone in East Lothian.

Brown (91) *English* and *Lowland Scottish.* Derived in most cases as a nickname for someone who was 'brown-haired' or 'brown-skinned'. An Anglo-Norman family of this name settled in Ireland in the 12th century. *Socts Gaelic.* At least two septs, one meaning son of the judge and the other meaning son of the brown lad, had their names anglicised to Brown. On their outlawing by the Crown in the 17th century one of the names adopted by members of Clan Lamont was Brown.

Browne (24) See Brown. Browne tends to be more common in the South of Ireland.

Browse (1) Only recorded in Derry in the Northern Ireland phone book.

Bruce (4) *Scottish.* Derived from a place name in Normandy this clan traces its descent from Sir Robert de Brus, an 11th century Norman Knight. In the 12th century they were granted the Lordship of Annandale in Dumfriesshire. It was the 7th Lord of Annandale, Robert the Bruce who at Bannockburn in 1314 secured Scotland's independence from England.

Bryans (1) Can be of *English, Scottish* or *Irish* origin. In England and Scotland it derived from the Celtic personal name Brian which was introduced into Britain with the 11th century Norman invasion. In Ireland O'Brien (See O'Brien) and Byrne (See Byrne) sometimes became Bryan.

Bryce (4) A variant of Breslin. See Breslin.

Bryson (7) *Irish.* The County Donegal septs of Breslin (See Breslin) and O'Morison (See Morrison) anglicised their names to Bryson.

Buchanan (17) *Scottish.* This clan takes its name from the lands of Buchanan in Stirlingshire. It was founded by a branch of the O'Kanes of Derry who settled in Argyll in 1016. (See O'Kane).

Buckley (1) *English.* Derived from a number of place names meaning goat clearing. *Irish.* A sept of this name originated in County Offaly.

Buick (1) *English.* Derived from the place names of Bewick in Northumberland and North Yorkshire, meaning bee farm.

Burgess (2) *English* and *Scottish.* Derived from an occupational name which referred to a citizen or freeman of a city.

Burke (26) *English.* Derived from a local name for a fortification. In Ireland the Burkes, who came to be regarded as a great gaelic sept, trace their descent from William de Burgo, a Norman knight from Suffolk who invaded Ireland with Henry II in 1171 and received the earldom of Ulster.

Burnett (4) *English* and *Scottish.* The name has various origins including: a nickname meaning brownish; an occupational name for a seller of brown cloth; and a variant of the Old English personal name Bernard. Burnett has been recorded in Ireland since the mid-17th century.

Burney (1) See McBurney.

Burns (25) *Scots Gaelic.* Originally a Clan Campbell sept who took their name from Burnhouse in Argyllshire. In addition Scottish McBurney (See McBurney) and Irish O'Byrne (See Byrne) were anglicised to Burns.

Burnside (8) *Scottish.* Derived from a local name for someone who lived by a stream. In addition there were three villages of this name in Fife, Nairn and Kincardine. Burnside has been recorded in County Derry since the early 17th century.

Burrow (1) *English.* Derived from a local name for someone who lived by a hill or burial mound. It was recorded in Ulster from the 17th century.

Burton (8) *English.* Derived from a number of place names, which are most frequent in the Midlands and North of England, meaning fort-settlement.

Busby (1) *English* and *Scottish.* Derived from a North Yorkshire place name which was recorded in the Domesday Book of 1086 and from the lands of Busby in Renfrewhire.

Butcher (1) *English* and *Scottish.* Derived from the occupational name for a butcher or slaughterer. It was recorded in Ireland from the 13th century.

Butler (1) *English* and *Scottish.* Derived originally from an occupational name for the servant in charge of the butts or casks of wine. This wine steward was regarded as the chief servant in a medieval household. In Ireland the Butlers, Earls of Ormond, trace their descent from Theobald Fitzwalter who accompanied Henry II to Ireland in 1170 and who, in 1177, was created "Chief Butler" (i.e. Overlord) of Ireland.

Byers (1) *English* and *Scottish.* Derived either from a local name for someone who lived by a cattleshed or from a number of place names such as the lands of Byres in East Lothian.

Byrne (2) *Irish.* This powerful sept established themselves in the Wicklow mountains after being driven out of County Kildare by the Normans. Some of those who settled in Ulster in the 17th century anglicised their name to Burns. (See Burns).

Byron (3) *English.* Derived either from a local name for someone who lived by a cattleshed or as an occupational name for a cowman. In Ireland Beirne (See Beirne) and Byrne (See Byrne) sometimes became Byron.

C

Cadden (5) *Irish.* This County Armagh sept were hereditary tenants of church lands in that county. The name frequently became McAdam (See McAdams).

Cahill (1) *Irish.* There were a number of septs of this name. As McCahill the name was particularly associated with Counties Donegal and Cavan.

Cahoon (1) See Colhoun.

Cairns (19) *Scottish.* Derived from the lands of Cairns in Midlothian the name became well established in Galloway from the early 15th century.

Caldwell (19) Can be of *English, Scottish* or *Irish* origin. In England and Scotland it derived from a number of place names meaning cold spring or stream. In Ireland at least two septs, namely Horish of Tyrone and Cullivan of Cavan, anglicised their names to Caldwell.

Callaghan (12) *Irish.* There were two septs of this name, of which the more powerful one was based in County Cork. The majority of Ulster Callaghans, however, descend from the Kelaghan sept whose stronghold was outside Fivemiletown in County Tyrone.

Callan (10) *Irish.* It may be a variant of McCallion (See McCallion) or a contracted form of O'Callan, a County Monaghan sept. Some may have Scots gaelic origins as a variant of McAllen. (See Allen).

Callen (3) See Callan.

Cambell (1) See Campbell.

Cambridge (1) *English.* Derived from the place name Cambridge, meaning bridge over the River Cam. *Scots Gaelic.* As a variant of McCambridge this surname was associated with the Mull of Kintyre.

Cameron (1) *Scots Gaelic.* Derived from a nickname meaning crooked nose this clan, whose stronghold was at Loch Eil in Inverness-shire, was described "as fiercer than fierceness itself". *Lowland Scottish.* Derived from a number of place names in Fife, Midlothain and Stirlingshire meaning crooked hill.

Cammack (1) *Scottish.* It was first recorded as a surname here in the late 16th century.

Campbell (110) *Scots Gaelic.* Derived from a nickname meaning crooked mouth the Campbells of Argyll grew in power through the 17th century at the expense of the MacDonalds, Lords of the Isles. Most Ulster Campbells are of this connection. The galloglasses or mercenary soldiers of Clan Campbell settled in Donegal from the 15th century.

Irish. A County Tyrone sept whose name meant son of the battle chief was anglicised to Campbell.

Canavan (9) *Irish.* Derived from a byname meaning little black-headed one this County Galway sept were hereditary physicians to the O'Flahertys.

Canney (2) See Canny.

Canning (31) *English.* Most County Derry Cannings descend from the Cannings of Garvagh who came to Ulster in 1615 from Warwickshire as agents to the estate of the London Company of Ironmongers. Canning was derived from the Wiltshire place name of Cannings. Occasionally the County Donegal sept name of Cannon became Canning.

Canny (2) *Irish.* The County Mayo sept of O'Canny and the County Clare sept of McCanny were shortened to Canny. In Tyrone Canny can be a variant of McCann (See McCann).

Carey (8) *Irish.* Carey is now widespread as the anglicised form of a number of names such as McCary, Crean, Currane, O'Keary and Kerin. It may in some instances be a variant of the Welsh name Carew which was derived from a number of place names meaning fort-hill.

Cargill (3) *Scottish.* Derived from the lands of Cargill in East Perthshire it was first recorded as a surname there in the 13th century. In County Donegal McGarrigle sometimes became Cargill.

Carland (1) A variant of Carlin. see Carlin.

Carley (1) *Irish.* The County Roscommon sept of McCarrelly was anglicised to Carley. In County Wexford an English family of this name settled here.

Carlin (63) *Irish.* Tracing their descent from Eoghan, son of the 5th century Niall of the Nine Hostages and originating in the Laggan district of County Donegal the Carlins or O'Carolans were the leading sept of Clan Dermot who were very powerful in the neighbourhood of Derry during the 11th and 12th centuries. Although eventually overrun by the O'Kanes the parish name of Glendermot is a reminder of their former prominence and the townland name of Lismacarrol, meaning the fort of the sons of Carroll, as a former base.

Carlisle (1) *English* and *Scottish.* Derived from the place name of Carlisle in Cumberland the surname was first recorded in Scotland around 1200. The Carlisles were one of the smaller riding clans of the Scottish Borders.

Carmichael (2) *Scottish.* Derived from the lands of Carmichael in Lanarkshire. The family granted these lands adopted it as their surname in the early 13th century. The Carmichaels were a sept of Clan Stewart.

Carr (9) Can be of *English, Scottish* or *Irish* origin. In England it derived as a local name for someone who lived by a marsh. In Scotland it is a variant of Kerr (See Kerr) while in Ireland a number of Ulster septs, such as Kilcarr of Donegal and Carry of Armagh, anglicised their name to Carr.

Carrigan (1) A variant of Corrigan. See Corrigan.

Carroll (3) *Irish.* The County Offaly and County Monaghan septs of O'Carroll and the County Derry sept of McCarroll, who were renowed as musicians in the 14th century, were shortened to Carroll.

Carruthers (10) *Scottish.* Derived from the lands of Carruthers in Dumfreisshire it was first recorded as a surname in the early 14th century. In 1587 they were recorded as one of the unruly clans of the Scottish Borders.

Carson (5) *Scottish.* Especially prominent in Dumfreisshire and Kirkcudbrightshire this surname first came to Ulster, and to Tyrone in particular, with the 17th century plantation.

Carter (1) *English.* Derived as an occupational name for a transporter of goods. In some cases Scottish MacArthur (See McArthur) became McCarter or Carter. The name has been recorded in Ireland since the 14th century.

Cartin (3) *Irish.* Meaning son of Art this County Down sept were sub-lords to the McGuinnesses. Cartin amd McCartin have been recorded as variants of Scottish McCartney (See McCartney).

Carton (5) See Cartin.

Casey (22) *Irish.* There were at least seven distinct septs of the name. The County Fermanagh sept of O'Casey were hereditary tenants of the church lands of Devenish. Other septs of the name originated in Counties Cork, Dublin, Limerick, Mayo, Monaghan and Roscommon.

Cassidy (53) *Irish.* A County Fermanagh sept who were hereditary physicians to the Maguires.

Cathcart (4) *Scottish.* Derived from the lands of Cathcart in Renfrewshire. The first known bearer of the surname came to Scotland with Walter, the High Steward, in the 12th century. The royal house of Stewart trace their descent from this Walter (See Stewart).

Cathers (2) *Scottish.* Derived from the place name of Catter or Cather in Dunbartonshire it was first recorded as a surname in the early 16th century.

Catterson (2) A variant of Cathers. See Cathers.

Cauley (2) A variant of McAuley. See McAuley.

Cavanagh (9) See Kavanagh.

Ceulemans (1) Originating in *Belgium* this name is only recorded in Derry in the Northern Ireland phone book.

Chada (10) Arriving in Derry in 1930 the Chadas were the first Indians to settle in Ireland. The original bearer of the name came to Derry via Kenya where he was a self-taught mechanic. He arrived in Derry on board a ship which had sailed from Mombasa via Marseilles. Settling in Derry the Chadas built up a thriving footwear and drapery business which by 1957 was employing 25 people. By 1957 the Indian community in the city stood at 50.

Chadwick (1) *English.* Derived from a number of place names in the North and Midlands of England meaning dairy farm.

Chambers (17) *English* and *Scottish.* Derived from an occupational name for a chamber attendant it was first recorded as a surname in Scotland in the 13th century.

Channing (2) Perhaps derived from Chanin which was a known variant of the female names Hannah and Anna or as a variant of Canning (See Canning).

Channon (2) *English.* Chiefly found in the West Country as a variant of Cannon which derived as a nickname for a clergyman living in a communal house of clergy. In County Donegal Cannon was adopted as an anglicisation by one of its septs.

Chapell (1) *English* and *Scottish.* Derived from a local name for someone who lived near a chapel it was first recorded as a surname in Scotland in the early 14th century.

Chapman (2) *English* and *Scottish.* Derived from an occupational name for a merchant or trader. In Scotland the surname was found mainly in the Lothians and Perthshire.

Charles (1) *English* and *Scottish.* Derived from an Old French personal name which was introduced to Britain by the Normans. Under Stewart patronage it became a popular name in Scotland in the 16th century.

Charlesson (1) *Scottish.* Meaning son of Charles (See Charles) this form of the name was associated with Caithness.

Chauhan (1) Originating from the State of Rajasthan in Northern India this name came to Ireland in 1958 via East Africa.

Cheetham (1) *English.* Derived from the Lancashire place name, meaning wood homestead.

Cheshire (1) *English.* Derived from the county name of Cheshire in North-West England this surname originally referred to someone who came from that county.

Cheung (3) This *Chinese* surname is now found throughout Northern Ireland. In Eire there are 9 listings of the name in the telephone directories while in Northern Ireland there are 25 entries, including 6 in Belfast, 3 in Limavady, 3 in Derry and 2 in Larne.

Christie (2) *Scottish.* Meaning either little Christopher or little Christian this surname was very common in Fife. In Argyllshire Gilchrist, meaning son the the servant of Christ, was anglicised to Christie.

Christy (1) See Christie.

Chrysfidis (1) Originating from the town of Salonica in Northern Greece this name came to Ireland in 1972.

Clancey (1) *Irish.* There were two distinct septs of this name: The County Clare sept were a branch of the McNamaras while in North Leitrim the Clancys were chiefs of Rosclogher.

Clark (4) See Clarke.

Clarke (33) Can be of *English, Scottish* or *Irish* origin. In England and Lowland Scotland Clark derived as an occupational name for a clerk or cleric while in Ireland and Highland Scotland Clark was a further anglicisation of O'Clery and McCleary (See McCleery).

Cleary (1) A variant of McCleary. See McCleery.

Clerkin (2) *Irish.* As well as being a County Limerick sept, Clerkin is a recorded variant of McCleary (See McCleery).

Clews (1) *English.* This is a variant of Clough which derived from a local name for someone who lived near a ravine or deep valley. Clews is particularly associated with Derbyshire.

Clifford (20) *English.* Derived from various place names meaning slope-ford. At the end of the 16th century a family of this name settled in County Sligo. *Irish.* The County Kerry sept name of Cluvane was widely changed to Clifford.

Clinton (1) *English* and *Scottish.* Derived from place names in Oxfordshire and Northamptonshire families of this name settled in Ireland in the late 12th century. In Scotland Clinton was usually a shortened form of McClinton which in turn was a variant of McClintock (See McClintock).

Cloete (2) This name of South African origin is only recorded in the telephone directories of Ireland in Derry.

Coates (1) *English* and *Scottish.* Derived from a local name for someone who lived in a cottage. In Scotland it was a variant of Coutts which was derived from the Aberdeenshire place name of Cults. A family of this name settled in Tyrone shortly after the plantation of Ulster in the early 17th century.

Cochrane (1) *Scottish.* Derived from the place name of Cochrane near Paisley in Renfrewshire the Cochranes were a sept of Clan Donald.

Cokayne (1) *English.* Derived from a nickname for an idle dreamer a family of this name has been established in Derbyshire since the mid-12th century.

Colclough (3) *English.* Derived from the place name of Cowclough in

Lancashire, meaning Cola's ravine this name was recorded in County Wexford in the 16th century.

Cole (8) Can be of *English, Scottish* or *Irish* origin. In England Cole was a shortened form of Nicholas and a family of this name settled in Fermanagh during the plantation. In Scotland McDougall was sometimes anglicised to Cole (See Duggal) while in Ireland the County Donegal sept of McCool was anglicised to Cole.

Coleman (1) *English.* Derived as occupational names either for a charcoal burner or for a servant to a person named Cole (See Cole). *Irish.* Coleman was also the name of a sept which originated in County Sligo. At a later date a branch migrated to Counties Cork and Kerry.

Coles (1) See Cole.

Colhoun (31) *Scottish.* This clan takes its name from the lands of Colquhoun in Dunbartonshire which they acquired in the 13th century. In the 16th and 17th centuries they were involved in a bitter feud with the McGregors.

Coll (5) *Scots Gaelic.* A galloglass or mercenary soldier family of Argyllshire belonging to Clan Donald. Members of this sept settled in Donegal in the 16th century.

Collins (22) *English.* Derived from the Christian name Colin which in turn was derived from the popular medieval name Nicholas. *Irish.* Cullen was sometimes further anglicised to Collins (See Cullen).

Colville (1) *Scottish.* Derived from Colleville in Normandy the name was first recorded in Scotland in the mid-12th century.

Comey (1) *Irish.* This name was associated with the ancient kingdom of Breffny in County Cavan.

Conaghan (16) *Irish.* Associated with West Derry and East Donegal this sept's name was further anglicised to Cunningham (See Cunningham).

Concannon (13) *Irish.* Tracing their descent from the 10th century Cuceannan this sept were chiefs of Kilkerrin, County Galway from the 11th to the 15th centuries.

Condren (2) See Condron.

Condron (1) *Irish.* This sept, also called Conran, originated in County Offaly and by the 17th century the name was common in the adjoining counties of Leix and Kildare.

Coney (1) *English.* Derived as a local name for someone who lived by a water channel. *Irish.* A variant of Cooney. (See Cooney).

Conn (1) *Scottish.* This old Aberdeenshire name is claimed to be a branch of Clan Donald. *Irish.* Conn can be a shortened form of a variety of names such as Connell (See O'Connell), Connolly (See Connolly) and Connor (See O'Connor).

Connelly (1) See Connolly.

Connolly (6) *Irish.* There were three distinct septs of this name: In Galway they were a branch of the O'Maddens; in Monaghan they were a branch of the Southern O'Neill and one of the four tribes of Tara; while in County Cork Connollys were sub-lords to the O'Donovans.

Connor (12) See O'Connor.

Conway (6) *Welsh.* This common Welsh name is derived from the River Conway. *Irish.* Several septs, including McConomy (See McConomy), anglicised their name to Conway.

Conwell (3) *Irish.* Chiefly found in Donegal it is a variant of McConville. This sept originated in the ancient territory of Oriel which incorporated Counties Armagh and Monaghan.

Cook (1) See Cooke.

Cooke (19) *English.* Derived from an occupational name for a cook. *Scots Gaelic.* As an abbreviated form of McCooke they were a Clan Donald sept of Kintyre and Arran.

Cooley (16) *Irish.* In the North-West Cooley is usually a variant of Cowley (See Cowley).

Cooney (1) *Irish.* This sept originated in County Tyrone but by the mid-13th century they had migrated westwards and settled in Counties Roscommon and Sligo.

Cooper (5) *English* and *Scottish.* Derived from the occupational name for a maker and repairer of wooden barrels and casks. In Scotland, where the name occurs in every county, Cooper was also derived from the Fife place name of Cupar.

Copeland (1) *English* and *Scottish.* Derived from place names in Cumberland and Northumberland meaning bought land as distinct from land held by feudal tenure. The surname arrived early in

Scotland and even found its way to the Orkney Islands by the mid-15th century.

Corbett (3) *English* and *Scottish.* This Norman name meaning raven was probably used as a nickname for someone with dark hair or dark complexion. In the early 12th century a Shropshire family of the name settled in the Scottish Borders.

Corkhill (1) This shortened from of McCorkell was particularly associated with the Isle of Man (See McCorkell).

Corlett (1) *Isle of Man.* A branch of Scottish McLeod (See McLeod) who trace their descent from Leod who was the son of Olaf, King of Mann and the Isles.

Cormie (1) *Scottish.* Originating in Letham in Fifeshire this name came to Derry around 1890 via Glasgow.

Cornwath (1) *Scottish.* Derived from the lands of Carnwath in Lanarkshire it was first recorded as a surname in Edinburgh in the early 16th century.

Corr (6) *Irish.* This sept originated in Counties Tyrone and Fermanagh. In addition Corry (See Corry) was sometimes further anglicised to Corr.

Corrigan (1) *Irish.* A County Fermanagh sept of the same stock as the Maguires.

Corry (3) *Irish.* The South Derry name of Corr and the Fermanagh sept of McCorry, who were a branch of the Maguires, were also known as Corry. In addition the O'Corrys were one of the septs of Clan Dermot (See Carlin). *Scottish.* Derived from the Dumfriesshire place name of Corrie. The McCorrys were a sept of Clan Macquarrie of Mull.

Cosgrove (7) *Irish.* In Ulster four distinct septs anglicised their name to Cosgrove: two with origins in Monaghan, one in Armagh and the other in South Fermanagh. This name was also anglicised to McCusker (See McCusker).

Coskery (1) A variant of Cosgrove. See Cosgrove.

Cossum (2) *English.* This name was established in Hastings in Sussex by the early 17th century.

Costello (1) *English.* Tracing their descent from a 12th century Norman, Gilbert de Nangle this family adopted the name Costello and became a great gaelic sept in County Mayo where they constantly feuded with the McDermotts. In Counties Derry and Donegal the County Tyrone sept name of Cushely sometimes became Costello.

Couchman (1) *English.* Derived either from the occupational name for a maker of beds or as a nickname for a lazy man.

Coulson (1) A variant of Cole. See Cole.

Coulter (7) *Irish.* This County Down sept gave its name to Ballyculter. *Scottish.* Derived from the Lanarkshire place name of Coulter.

Coupe (2) A variant of Cooper (See Cooper) found in Yorkshire and Lancashire.

Coups (1) A variant of Cooper. See Cooper.

Courtney (1) *Irish.* The County Kerry sept of Curnane and the Ulster sept of McCourt (See McCourt) were further anglicised to Courtney. *English.* Derived either from the place name of Courtenay in Normandy or from a nickname for someone with a 'short nose'.

Cowan (8) *Scots Gaelic.* There were Cowan septs attached to Clans Dougall, Colquhon and Donald. In addition many Colhouns (See Colhoun) assumed this name. *Irish.* The County Armagh sept of McCone was anglicised to Cowan.

Cowey (1) *Irish.* A variant of Coffey. Three distinct septs of this name originated in Counties Cork, Galway and Westmeath.

Cowley (3) This is a variant of McAuley. See McAuley.

Cox (1) *Irish.* The County Roscommon sept name of McQuilly was extensively translated to the English name Cox, especially in County Monaghan. In England Cox was frequently attached to a given name to create a new surname.

Coy (1) *English.* Derived from a nickname for a quiet and unassuming person. There is no evidence that McCoy was shortened to Coy (See Coy).

Coyle (116) *Irish.* Meaning son of the servant of Comgall this sept established itself in Mevagh Parish, County Donegal. An early form of the name was McIlhoyle. Furthermore Coyle has become confused with McCool (See McCool).

Crabtree (1) *English.* Derived as a local name for someone who lived by a crab-apple tree.

Cradden (1) Also recorded in Lisburn and Dublin in Irish telephone directories it is perhaps a variant of Crudden (See Crudden). At least three generations of Craddens have lived in Derry's Waterside.

Craig (30) *Scottish.* Derived from a local name for someone who lived near a crag or rock. By the 15th century this surname was common throughout Edinburgh and the Lowlands of Scotland.

Crane (1) *English* and *Scottish.* Derived from a nickname from the bird which would have referred to someome who was skinny and long-legged. *Irish.* Crane was a variant of O'Crean (See Cregan).

Crapp (2) *English.* Derived from an occupational name for a picker of vegetables or a reaper of corn.

Crawford (15) *Scottish.* Derived from the lands of Crawford in Lanarkshire it was first recorded as a surname in the mid-12th century. The Crawfords were a sept of Clan Lindsay.

Crawley (5) *Irish.* The County Armagh sept of McCrawley and the County Cork sept of O'Crowley were shortened to Crawley. *English.* Crowley and its variant Crawley were derived from a number of place names meaning crows' wood.

Cree (1) *Irish.* A variant of Cregan (See Cregan). *Scottish.* Recorded in Ayrshire and Glasgow Cree was probably a shortening of McCrae (See McCrae).

Cregan (8) *Irish.* A variant of the County Donegal sept name of O'Crean who can trace their descent from Eoghan, son of the 5th century Niall of the Nine Hostages.

Creighton (1) *Scottish.* Derived from the lands of Crichton in Midlothian, meaning border-farm it was first recorded as a surname in the early 12th century.

Crerand (1) There are only two references to this name in the Northern Ireland phone book.

Creswell (7) *English.* Derived from a number of place names meaning watercress spring.

Crichton (2) See Creighton.

Crilly (5) *Irish.* Originating in the ancient kingdom of Oriel, which comprised Counties Armagh and Monaghan, this sept were hereditary tenants of the church lands of Tamlaght in County Derry, hence the parish name of Tamlaght O'Crilly near Kilrea.

Crocker (2) *English* and *Scottish*. Derived from the occupational name for a potter it was recorded as a surname in Scotland in Lanarkshire in the mid-19th century.

Crockett (9) *English*. Derived from a nickname for someone with a distinctive hairstyle of large curls. *Scots Gaelic*. In Galloway Crocket was the anglicised form of a sept name which meant son of Richard.

Crompton (1) *English*. Derived from the Lancashire place name, meaning crooked settlement i.e. a settlement by a bend in a river or road.

Cross (8) *English* and *Scottish*. Derived from a local name for someone who lived near a stone cross at the side of a road. *Irish*. A shortened form of Crossan. See Crossan.

Crossan (21) *Irish*. Originally McCrossan there were two distinct septs of the name. The County Tyrone sept was the more numerous and it provided two Bishops of Raphoe in the 14th century. The Crossans of County Leix were hereditary poets to the O'Mores and O'Connors.

Crothers (2) *English*. Derived as an occupational name for a player of a stringed instrument. *Scottish*. A variant of Carruthers. See Carruthers.

Crowe (4) Can be of *English*, *Scottish* or *Irish* origin. In England and Scotland it derived from a nickname from the bird. It was recorded as a surname in Scotland in the late 15th century. In Ireland the County Clare sept of McEnchroe, who were sub-lords to the O'Deas, was anglicised to Crowe.

Crowley (2) See Crawley.

Cruickshank (4) *Scottish*. Derived either from a nickname for a man with a crooked leg or from the River Cruick in Kincardineshire this surname was associated with Aberdeenshire and Kincardineshire.

Crumley (10) *Irish*. This sept originated in Counties Derry and Donegal. In some cases it may be a variant of Crumlish. See Crumlish.

Crumlish (5) *Irish*. This sept, whose name originally meant descendant of the squint-eyed man, originated in County Donegal.

Crystal (1) *Scottish.* Derived either as a shortened form of the christian name Christopher or as a variant of McChrystal (See McChrystal). Crystal was a fairly commom surname in Aryshire in the 15th century and it was recorded in Counties Armagh and Tyrone from the 17th century.

Cuddy (1) *Irish.* This sept originated in County Kilkenny but the earliest reference to the name was in County Cork in the early 13th century. *English* and *Scottish.* Derived from a shortened form of the personal name Cudbert, which was the common pronounciation of Cuthbert in Lowland Scotland and the North of England (See Cuthbert).

Culbert (1) *Scottish.* Derived from the Old English name of Colbert this surname was associated with Fifeshire.

Cullen (9) *Irish.* Two distinct septs of this name originated in Counties Donegal and Monaghan. *Scottish.* Derived from the burgh of Cullen in Banffshire.

Cullin (1) See Cullen.

Cully (1) A variant of McCullagh. See McCullagh.

Cummings (5) *Scottish.* Derived from an Old French personal name this clan lost its land and titles when Robert the Bruce secured the throne of Scotland in the early 14th century. They, however, remained strong in their Northeast homeland of Elgin, Banff and Aberdeen.

Cunningham (27) *Scottish.* This clan takes its name from the district of Cunningham in Ayrshire. During the 17th century plantation many Cunninghams settled in Donegal. *Irish.* Cunninghan was the adopted anglicisation of a number of septs such as McCunnigan of Donegal and Conaghan of Derry.

Curley (5) *Irish.* This variant of the County Armagh sept name of Turley was mainly found in Counties Galway and Roscommon.

Curran (46) *Irish.* There were several distinct septs of this name. In Galway they were a branch of the O'Maddens while in Waterford and Tipperary the Currans were a big sept by the 17th century. The name is numerous in Derry today because a Curran sept also originated in Donegal.

Currie (2) See Curry.

Curry (14) *Irish.* There were two distinct septs of this name; one originated in County Clare, the other in Westmeath. *Scots Gaelic.* Septs of this name, meaning son of Murdock, were branches of Clan Donald and Clan MacPherson. It may also be a variant of Corrie (See Corry).

Curtis (6) *English.* Derived from a nickname for 'a courteous, well-bred person' this surname was recorded in Ireland from the 13th century.

Cusack (6) *English.* Derived from the place name of Cussac in France this name was introduced to Ireland following the Norman invasion in 1172. From their base in County Meath they became regarded as one of the great gaelic septs.

Cuthbert (1) *English* and *Scottish.* Derived from an Old English personal name which was popularised by the 7th century Saint of the name who was Bishop of Lindisfarne. In Scotland the county of Kirkcudbright was named after the saint. Cuthbert became a wide-spread surname throughout the Lothians of Scotland and the North of England.

Cuthbertson (1) This variant of Cuthbert (See Cuthbert) simply means son of Cuthbert.

D

Dakin (1) *English.* Meaning little David it was first recorded as a surname in the late 13th century. David was a popular christian name in the Middle Ages owing to the biblical king of the name. In Scotland two King Davids who reigned in the 12th and 14th centuries popularised the name there.

Dale (1) *English.* Derived from the local name for someone who lived in a valley. It was recorded as a surname in Scotland from the late 14th century.

Dalton (3) *English.* Derived from a place name, written d'Autun, in Normandy this name was introduced to Ireland following the 12th century Norman invasion. Settling in Meath and later spreading into Cork and Tipperary the Daltons came to be regarded as one of the great gaelic septs.

Daly (17) *Irish.* This sept originated in County Westmeath but later migrated to County Cavan where they became hereditary poets to the O'Reillys.

Dalzall (1) See Dalzell.

Dalzell (4) *Scottish.* Derived from a place name in the Clyde Valley recorded as Dalyell in the year 1200, meaning field-white. Dalzell was recorded in County Down from the 17th century.

Damijo (1) Originating in the town of Warri on the delta of the River Niger in Nigeria this name came to Ireland in 1984.

Darby (1) *English.* Derived from the town of Derby in Derbyshire, meaning deer farm. A family of the name settled in County Leix in the 16th century. In Ireland the County Donegal sept name of Dermond was sometimes made Darby.

Darcy (2) *English.* Derived from a place name, written d'Arcy, in Normandy a family of the name established themselves in County Meath in the mid-14th century. *Irish.* Two septs originating in the Mayo/Galway area and in County Waterford anglicised their name to Darcy. Descendants from the Darcys of Mayo became one of the "Tribes of Galway". Strictly speaking d'Arcy denotes Norman origin and Darcy Irish origin.

Darke (1) *English.* Derived from a nickname for someone 'with dark hair' or 'a dark complexion'. This surname is commonest in the West Country.

Darragh (1) *Irish.* This County Antrim sept name was sometimes anglicised to Oakes. *Scots Gaelic.* A variant of Darroch who were a branch of Clan Donald.

Davey (1) *English.* This shortened form of David (See Dakin) is chiefly found in Devon and Cornwall.

Davidson (6) *Scottish.* Meaning son of David (See Dakin) this clan was originally part of the Clan Chattan confederation with lands in Perthshire and Inverness-shire. The Davidsons were also one of the smaller riding clans of the Scottish Borders. *Irish.* In some cases McDaid (See McDaid) was anglicised to Davidson.

Davies (2) A variant of Davidson. See Davidson.

Davis (13) As well as being a variant of Davidson (See Davidson) Davis was also a Welsh name which meant son of Davy.

Davison (3) See Davidson.

Dawson (2) Can be of *English, Scottish* or *Irish* origin. Originally meaning son of David (See Dakin) this surname became widespread in Northern England. In Scotland the Dawsons were a sept of Clan Davidson in South Inverness-shire while in Ireland Doran (See Doran) was in some cases anglicised to Dawson.

Day (2) *English.* Derived either from a shortened form of David (See Dakin) or from an occupational name for a dairymaid or dairyman. *Irish.* The County Clare sept of O'Dea was anglicised to Day.

Dazell (1) See Dalzell.

De Glinn (1) *English.* Derived from the manor of Glynn near Bodmin in Cornwall where Hubert de Glin was farming in the year 1000. Glin in Cornwall and Glyn in Wales are local names for someone who lived in a valley.

Deane (8) *English.* Derived from a local name for someone living in a valley. A family of this name settled in County Kilkenny in the 13th century. *Irish.* Derived from the gaelic word for a dean septs of this name originated in Counties Donegal, Roscommon and Tipperary.

Deans (3) *Scottish.* This variant of Dean (See Deane) was particularly common around Hawick in the Scottish Borders in the 16th century.

Deany (1) *English.* This variant of Denny was derived from the christian name Dennis. A family so-named came from England in the 16th century and settled in County Derry. *Irish.* A variant of Deeney. See Deeney.

Deegan (1) *Irish.* This sept originated in County Leix and at the time of the plantation they lost their lands to Sir Charles Coote who gave his name to Cootehill in County Cavan.

Deehan (14) *Irish.* In a few cases this sept with origins in County Derry have had their name changed to Dickson (See Dickson).

Deeney (19) *Irish.* Originating in County Donegal this sept was strongly represented in the priesthood in the Diocese of Raphoe from the 15th century.

Deeny (4) See Deeney.

Deery (25) *Irish.* Originating in County Derry this sept were hereditary stewards of the church lands in Derry city itself. The County Donegal sept name of O'Derry has to a large extent been absorbed into Deery.

Del Pinto (1) This is just one of at least eleven new surnames established in Derry city in the early 20th century by a thriving Italian community. The other names included Battisti, Caffola, Cassoni, Centra, Corrieri, Fiorentini, Forte, Macari, Vaccaro and Yannarelli.

Delahunt (1) *Irish.* Originating in County Offaly this sept was a branch of the O'Carrolls.

Delaney (2) *Irish.* Originating in County Leix this sept's name which meant Black Slaney refers to the River Slaney.

Delpinto (2) See Del Pinto.

Denning (1) *Irish.* As a variant of Dinneen this sept originated in County Cork.

Dennison (2) *English* and *Scottish.* Derived from the given name Dennis which was popular in Britain from the 12th century onwards. In Scotland Denniston derived from the Renfrewshire place name of Danzielstoun.

Dentith (1) *English.* Derived from a nickname meaning 'pleasure' this surname was most common in Lancashire.

Desmonds (5) *Irish.* Originating in South-West Cork, which was formerly known as Desmond, this sept migrated and settled in North and East Cork.

Devenney (6) *Irish.* Two distinct septs of this name originated in Ulster; one in County Down, the other in Donegal. The name has become confused with Devane of Galway and Kerry and, in some cases, with Devine (See Devine).

Devenny (4) See Devenney.

Devine (50) Irish. Tracing their descent from the 10th century King of the ancient Kingdom of Oriel the Devines were a leading County Fermanagh sept until their power was checked by the O'Neills and the Maguires in the 15th century.

Devir (1) *Irish.* This surname is still largely to be found in County Donegal where the sept originated and gained some prominence in the medieval period.

Devlin (22) *Irish.* This County Tyrone sept, who ruled over territory on the west shore of Lough Neagh, trace their descent from Eoghan, son of the 5th century Niall of the Nine Hostages. The chief of the sept was hereditary swordbearer to O'Neill.

Diamond (4) *Irish.* This sept originated in East Derry where they were hereditary stewards of church lands.

Dickie (1) *Scottish.* This variant of Dickson (See Dickson) was first recorded in Glasgow in 1504.

Dickinson (1) This variant of Dickson (See Dickson) is most common in the North and Midlands of England.

Dickson (4) *Scottish.* Derived from a shortened form of the Germanic personal name Richard which was popularised in Britain by the Normans. Dickson is usually regarded as Scottish and Dixon as English. The Dicksons or Dixons (See Dixon) were one of the riding clans of the Scottish Borders. *Irish.* In County Derry Dickson has been used as an anglicisation of Deehan (See Deehan).

Dillon (12) *English.* Derived from the Germanic personal name Dillo it was introduced into England by the Normans in the 11th century and then to Ireland in the 12th century. The Dillons acquired vast territories in County Westmeath and, in time, became regarded as a great gaelic sept. In some cases the County Limerick sept name of Dillane was made Dillon.

Dingley (1) *English.* Derived from a Northamptonshire place name, meaning a clearing in a wooded hollow.

Dinsmore (5) *Scottish.* Derived from the lands of Dundemore in Fife a family of this name emigrated to County Antrim in the early 17th century and from there emigrated to Londonderry, New Hampshire in 1723. Dinsmore is mainly found in Counties Derry and Donegal.

Diver (3) See Devir.

Divers (1) See Devir.

Divin (4) A variant of Devine. See Devine.

Dixon (6) This surname is usually regarded as the English spelling of Dickson (See Dickson). In the Scottish Borders, however, it was traditional to use both forms of the name.

Doak (4) *Scottish.* A variant of Doig which originally meant son of the servant of Cadoc. It was first recorded as a surname in Scotland from the late 15th century.

Dobbin (1) Meaning little Robert Dobbin was derived from the Germanic personal name Robert which was introduced into England by the Normans. The surname was first recorded in Ulster at Carrickfergus in 1400, and between 1571 and 1661 they provided eight mayors of this County Antrim town.

Dobbins (6) This surname originally meant son of little Robert. See Dobbin.

Dobson (1) *English* and *Scottish*. Meaning son of Dobb it is another shortened form of Robert (See Dobbin). It was recorded as a surname in the Scottish Borders in the mid-16th century.

Dodd (1) *English* and *Scottish*. Derived from an Old English personal name an English family of this name settled in County Sligo in the late 16th century. In some cases Duddy (See Duddy) became Dodd.

Doherty (469) *Irish*. By far the most popular name in Derry. Together with O'Doherty this name is listed 523 times in the Foyle Community Directory. This County Donegal sept, which originated in Raphoe but settled in Inishowen from the 14th century, can trace their lineage to Conall Gulban, son of the 5th century High King of Ireland, Niall of the Nine Hostages. They ruled Inishowen until the arrival of an English army at Derry in 1600. An O'Doherty-led rebellion, which included the ransacking of Derry in 1608, helped pave the way for the plantation of Ulster.

Dolan (3) *Irish*. This sept which originated in Counties Galway and Roscommon later moved north into Fermanagh and Cavan.

Donaghey (24) This anglicisation of McDonagh (See McDonagh) established itself in Counties Derry and Tyrone.

Donaghy (24) See Donaghey.

Donald (1) A variant of McDonald. See McDonald.

Donaldson (4) *Scottish*. An anglicisation of McDonald which was first noted in Edinburgh in the 14th century. See McDonald.

Donegan (2) Irish. There were at least four distinct septs of the name; with origins in Counties Cork, Monaghan, Sligo and Westmeath.

Donnell (1) A shortened form of either McDonnell (See McDonnell) or O'Donnell (See O'Donnell).

Donnelly (43) *Irish*. As a branch of the O'Neills this sept can trace its lineage to Eoghan, son of the 5th century Niall of the Nine Hostages. Originating in County Donegal they later migrated to Tyrone where their chief was hereditary marshall in O'Neill's army.

Donohoe (4) *Irish.* Stemming from the personal name Donagh (See McDonagh) septs of this name originated in County Cork, where they were a branch of the O'Mahonys, and in Cavan and Galway.

Dooher (2) *Irish.* This rather rare surname is found mainly in County Donegal.

Dooley (2) *Irish.* Originating in County Westmeath this sept migrated at an early date to County Offaly where they gained the right to inaugurate the O'Carrolls as Kings of Ely.

Doran (25) *Irish.* Originally one of the "Seven Septs of Leix" this sept established itself in Counties Armagh and Down.

Dorrian (5) A variant of Doran. See Doran.

Dorrity (3) A variant of Doherty. See Doherty.

Dougan (1) *Irish.* There were two distinguished septs of this name. In County Tipperary, in pre-Norman times, they were chiefs of "Roche's Country" while in County Galway the Dougans were sub-lords to the O'Kellys.

Dougherty (16) A variant of Doherty. See Doherty.

Douglas (9) *Scottish.* Taking their name from Douglas in Lanarkshire this clan played a prominent part in the struggle for Scottish independence at the turn of the 14th century. They even rivalled the Stewarts for the Kingship of Scotland. In the Scottish Borders the Douglases were one of the riding clans.

Dowds (1) *Irish.* Tracing their descent from Fiachra, brother of the 5th century Niall of the Nine Hostages, this sept at one time ruled over an extensive territory which included North Mayo and North-West Sligo. Their power was curtailed by the Norman invaders in the 13th century.

Dowling (1) A variant of Dolan. See Dolan.

Downey (28) *Irish.* There were two distinct septs of the name. In County Galway they were a branch of the O'Maddens while in County Down Muldowney was shortened to Downey. *Scots Gaelic.* Derived either from the lands of Duny or Downie in Angus or as a shortened form of McIldownie which meant son of the lord's servant.

Downing (1) *Irish.* A variant of Dinneen, the County Cork sept who were hereditary poets to the McCarthys. Downing can also be an English name with it being most common in Cornwall and Suffolk.

Downs (1) *English.* Derived from the local name for a low hill. *Irish.* It may be a variant of Dunn (See Dunn) or of a number of gaelic septs whose names were variously anglicised to Dwane, Duane, Devane and Downs.

Doyle (7) *Irish.* Found mainly in Wicklow, Wexford and Carlow this sept's name, meaning dark foreigner, was probably given to a descendant of one of the Norsemen or Vikings who settled on the sea coast of Ireland in pre-Norman times. In Ulster Doyle can be a variant of McDowell. See McDowell.

Drummond (1) *Scottish.* Derived from a number of place names meaning ridge this clan received lands in Perthshire for their support of Robert the Bruce at Bannockburn in 1314.

Duddy (42) *Irish.* This distinct sept, whose name in gaelic was the same as that of O'Dowd (See Dowds), originated in County Derry and anglicised their name to Duddy.

Dudgeon (1) *English* and *Scottish.* Derived from the occupational name for a turner or cutler it was recorded as a surname in Scotland from the early 16th century and in West Ulster since 1689.

Duff (2) *Irish.* This name is usually derived from a nickname meaning 'black'. It may also be a shortened form of the County Armagh sept name of Duffin and the County Tyrone sept name of McIlduff. *Scots Gaelic.* In Galloway McIlduff was shortened to Duff while in Fife Duff was a sept of Clan McDuff. (See McDuff).

Duffield (1) *English.* Derived from place names in Derbyshire and East Yorkshire, meaning open countryside frequented by doves.

Duffy (68) *Irish.* Two distinct septs of this name originated in Ulster; one in Monaghan who were based at Clontibret, the other in Donegal where they were hereditary tenants of the church lands of Templecrone. *Scots Gaelic.* A sept of Clan MacFie who trace their descent from Kenneth McAlpine, the 9th century King of Scots. Meaning 'son of the black one of peace' this clan's home was on the island of Colonsay in the Hebrides.

Duggal (1) *Scots Gaelic.* A variant of McDougall. Meaning son of the black foreigner this clan traces its descent from Duggal, the eldest son of Somerled, the 12th century Lord of Argyll. They acquired the lands of Lorn in Argyll. They came to Ireland as galloglasses or mercenary soldiers where their name became known as McDowell (See McDowell).

Duggan (1) See Dougan.

Dumigan (1) *Irish.* This spelling of the rare East Leinster name of Domegan was associated with County Down.

Dummion (1) It may be a variant of Dunnion. See Dunnion.

Duncan (6) *Scots Gaelic.* This is the Scottish form of the Irish personal name Donagh (See McDonagh). Members of Clan Robertson of Perthshire adopted this name after its 14th century chief Fat Duncan (See Roberts).

Dunleavy (1) *Irish.* An ancient Irish family who were driven from County Down by the Normans in the 12th century and settled in Donegal. *Scots Gaelic.* It can be a variant of McKinley. See McKinley.

Dunlop (19) *Scottish.* Derived from the lands of Dunlop in Ayrshire, meaning muddy hill it was first recorded as a surname in the mid-13th century. Dunlop became established in both Kintyre and North Antrim owing to 17th century plantations in both areas.

Dunn (17) *Irish.* This powerful sept originated in County Leix where they became lords of Iregan and noted opponents of English incursions in the mid-16th century. *Scottish.* They were one of the smaller riding clans on the English side of the Scottish Borders.

Dunne (10) See Dunn.

Dunnion (2) *Irish.* This is a variant of Downing (See Downing) found in Donegal.

Dunseath (1) *English* or *Scottish.* Dunseath has been recorded as a surname in Counties Tyrone and Antrim, especially in the Ballymena area, since the mid-17th century.

Dunseith (1) See Dunseath.

Durey (1) *Scottish.* Derived from the lands of Durie in Fife it was first recorded as a surname in the 13th century. *Irish.* In Counties

Leitrim and Roscommon there was a sept who anglicised their name to Durr and Dury.

Durkan (1) *Irish.* This County Sligo sept was a branch of the O'Haras and the name is now chiefly found in Counties Mayo and Sligo.

Durnin (3) *Irish.* This sept originated in Ulster where its name was usually recorded as Durnin in Counties Antrim and Down and as Durnion in Counties Donegal, Fermanagh and Tyrone.

Dykes (3) *Scottish.* Derived from the lands of Dykes in Strathclyde. This surname which is most common in Ayrshire and Lanarkshire would originally have referred to a person who lived by a ditch of dyke.

E

Eakin (1) A variant of Aiken. See Aiken.

Eames (1) *English.* This surname was originally applied to any person who acted as a guardian to a niece or nephew after their father died. The name was chiefly found in Bedfordshire and Somerset and it was recorded in Ulster from the mid-17th century.

Eaton (2) *English.* Derived from a number of place names meaning river or island settlement it was recorded in Ireland from the late 16th century.

Edgar (7) A variant of Adair. See Adair.

Edwards (10) *English* and *Scottish.* Meaning son of Edward it was derived from the given name made popular by two Kings of England, namely the 10th century Edward the Martyr and the 11th century Edward the Confessor.

El'Agnaf (1) In all of Ireland the only reference to El'Agnaf in the telephone directories is in Derry.

Elder (5) *English* and *Scottish.* Derived from a nickname to distinguish the elder of two bearers of the same forename it was recorded as a surname in Scotland from the early 15th century. In Ireland the surname is very much associated with Counties Derry and Donegal.

Elliott (13) *Scottish.* Derived from the Old English personal name Elwald the Elliotts were one of the great riding clans of the Scottish

Borders. During the 17th century plantation of Ulster they tended to settle in Fermanagh.

Ellis (3) *English* and *Scottish.* Derived from the christian name Elias which was popularised in Britain by the Crusaders it was first recorded as a surname in Ireland in the 13th century.

Emerson (2) *English.* Derived from a Germanic personal name which was introduced into England by the Normans in the 11th century.

England (1) A variant of English. See English.

English (5) *English* and *Scottish.* Derived as a name to distinguish Anglo-Saxons from other cultural groups such as the Celts in Scotland, the Vikings in Northern England or the Normans after their invasion of Southern England in 1066. It was recorded as a surname in Scotland from the early 13th century. Introduced into Ireland in the 13th century English, in time, became regarded as an Irish surname. In addition the County Donegal sept name of Gallogly was sometimes mistranslated to English.

Ennis (4) *Irish.* Ennis can either be a variant of McGuinness (See McGuinness) or of Hennessy. Septs of the latter name originated in North Offaly and Southwest Cork. *Scottish.* A sept of Clan Innes. This clan took its name from the lands of Innes in the Province of Moray.

Enright (1) *Irish.* Derived from a gaelic byname meaning attacker this surname is particularly associated with Counties Cork, Kerry and Limerick.

Ervine (1) See Irvine.

Etherson (1) *Scottish.* A variant of the surname Etherston which was first recorded in Roxburghshire in the late 13th century.

Evans (6) *Welsh.* Meaning son of John, Evans was the anglicised form of native Welsh Ieuan which was adopted when the Welsh began to apply a system of fixed surnames.

Ewing (1) *Scottish.* Derived from the personal name Ewen septs of this name were branches of Clans Dougall and MacLaren.

Eyre (1) *English.* Derived from a nickname for a man who was the heir to a title or fortune. English officials with this name were recorded in Ireland from the 16th century. In County Galway the Eyres, who came to Ireland with Cromwell in the mid-17th century, provided five sheriffs of the county between 1675 and 1809.

F

Fagan (2) *Irish.* Fagan is the Irish version of a surname of Norman origin. A family of the name acquired estates in County Meath in the 13th century. In some cases the County Louth sept name of Fegan became Fagan.

Fahy (4) *Irish.* Originating in County Galway this sept's base was at Loughrea where they held sway until the Cromwellian forfeitures of the mid-17th century.

Fairman (1) *English.* Derived from an occupational name for the servant of a person named Fair.

Falconer (3) A variant of Faulkner. See Faulkner.

Falker (1) It may be a variant of Faulkner. See Faulkner.

Faller (1) Originating in Schonwald, a small village in the Black Forest in Germany this name came to Derry in the 1870s. Faller means dweller at the waterfall which may refer to Treiberg in the Black Forest which is the highest waterfall (with a drop of 500') in Germany.

Fallon (2) *Irish.* This sept ruled over a territory near Athlone in County Roscommon. In Counties Armagh and Down the name is recorded as Falloon.

Fam (1) This Chinese name came to Derry from Hong Kong. There are no other references to Fam in the Irish Telephone directories.

Fan (1) Originating from a small mountain village outside Hong Kong this name came to Derry in the early 1960s.

Farrell (3) *Irish.* The ancestor, namely Feargal, who gave this sept its name was slain at the Battle of Clontarf in 1014. The Farrells originated in County Longford where they became Lords of Annaly.

Farrelly (1) *Irish.* Originating in County Cavan this sept were hereditary caretakers of Drumlane Abbey. In some cases Farrelly was further anglicised to Farley.

Farren (11) *Irish.* A sept of this name originated in the Inishowen peninsula in County Donegal. In addition the County Armagh sept name of Fearon tended to become Farron in Donegal.

Faulkner (17) *English* and *Scottish.* Derived from the occupational name for a trainer or keeper of falcons it was recorded as a surname in Scotland from 1200. Some Faulkners in Ireland may descend from one Nicholas Taylor, the 13th century 'Falconer' to Henry III.

Faulkner-Simpson (1) A double-barrelled name. See Faulkner and Simpson.

Fay (2) *English.* Derived from a number of place names in France meaning beech tree. An Anglo-Norman family of this name settled in Westmeath in the 12th century. In Ireland Fahy (See Fahy) and Foy (See Foy) sometimes became Fay.

Fealy (1) *Irish.* The West Cork sept of O'Fehilly, the County Kerry sept of O'Falvey and the North Roscommon sept of McFeely can also be known as Fealy.

Feeney (11) *Irish.* This sept originated in the parish of Easkey in County Sligo. A branch of this sept later established themselves in County Galway.

Feeny (1) See Feeney.

Fegan (4) See Fagan.

Fell (1) *English* and *Scottish.* Derived either from a local name for someone who lived by a mountain or from an occupational name for a furrier. In Scotland Fell is an old surname in Dundee.

Fenwick (1) *Northern English* and *Scottish.* Derived from places of that name in Ayrshire, Northumberland and West Yorkshire, meaning dairy farm on the fen or marsh. It was recorded as a surname in Ayr from the early 14th century.

Ferguson (35) *Scots Gaelic.* Clan Ferguson who claim descent from the 3rd century Irish King, Conn of the Hundred Battles, first settled on Kintyre. Since Fergus was a popular christian name the surname Ferguson spread all over Scotland, including the Province of Galloway which was the homeland of many Ulster Fergusons.

Ferris (12) *Irish.* The County Donegal sept of O'Ferry and the County Mayo sept of O'Fergus sometimes became anglicised as Ferris. *Scots Gaelic.* A branch of Clan Ferguson. See Ferguson.

Ferry (20) *Irish.* This County Donegal sept, who were followers of the McSweeneys, can trace their descent from Conall Gulban, son of the 5th century Niall of the Nine Hostages.

Fielding (3) *English.* Derived from a local name for someone who lived on land which had been cleared of forest but which had not been brought into cultivation. In Ireland the County Cork sept of Fehilly was often abbreviated to Feeley and sometimes anglicised to Field.

Fields (1) See Fielding.

Figini (1) In all of Ireland the only reference to Figini in the telephone directories is in Derry.

Finian (1) *Irish.* This sept which originated in County Mayo had established themselves in Counties Roscommon and Sligo by the 17th century.

Finlay (13) *Scots Gaelic.* The Finlays were a sept of Clan Farquharson and their name originally meant son of the fair hero. This name was also anglicised to McKinley. See McKinley.

Finn (2) *Irish.* Three distinct setps of the name originated in Counties Monaghan, Galway and Sligo. Today the name is cheifly found in County Cork.

Finnis (2) In all of Ireland the only reference to Finnis in the telephone directories is in Derry although Finnison is recorded in Warrenpoint and Finniston in Belfast. It is perhaps a variant of Scottish Finnieson which was recorded in Aberdeen in the early 15th century.

Fiorentini (5) Originating in Latina, 40 miles south of Rome in Italy this name came to Derry in 1911.

Fisher (4) *English* and *Scottish.* Derived from the occupational name for a fisherman. In Ireland, especially in the Glenties district of Donegal, gaelic Bradden has been anglicised to Fisher.

Fitzgibbon (1) *English.* Two families of this name, both tracing descent from 12th century Anglo-Norman invaders, settled in Ireland; one in County Limerick and the other, who were a branch of the Burkes, in County Mayo. Like most names of Norman origin they came in time to regard themselves as a gaelic sept.

Fitzpatrick (11) *Irish.* Meaning son of the devotee of Patrick this County Kilkenny sept assumed the Norman prefix Fitz (meaning son) in the 16th century. The name was in some cases anglicised to

Kilpatrick. See Kilpatrick.

Flack (1) *English* and *Scottish*. In England this surname, possibly derived from a nickname for a 'scruffily dressed person' is chiefly found in Cambridgeshire. In Scotland this name was formerly known as Affleck which was derived either from the lands of Auchinleck in Ayshire or from Affleck in Angus.

Flaherty (1) See O'Flaherty.

Flanagan (4) *Irish*. There were several septs of the name. A County Roscommon sept were a branch of the O'Connors, Kings of Connaught. In County Fermanagh Flanagans can trace their descent from Cairbre, son ot the 5th century Niall of the Nine Hostages while in County Monaghan they were a branch of the McDonnells.

Flannery (1) *Irish*. Two distinct septs of this name originated in Counties Mayo and Limerick.

Flay (1) The bearer of this name came to Derry in the mid-1980s from Wales. The family, however, was originally from Wiltshire in England.

Fleck (1) A variant of Flack. See Flack.

Fleming (23) *English* and *Scottish*. Meaning a native of Flanders many Flemings settled in Scotland and Wales in the 12th century. They first came to Ireland from Wales in the same century as the Norman invaders and they acquired considerable lands in County Meath. Many more, however, came from Scoltand with the 17th century plantation of Ulster.

Fletcher (1) *English* and *Scottish*. Derived from the occupational name for a maker of arrows. In Scotland septs of the name belonged to Clans Stewart of Appin, Campbell and MacGregor.

Flood (3) Can be of *English*, *Welsh* or *Irish* origin. In England it derived as a local name for someone who lived by a small stream. In Wales it was a variant of Lloyd while in Ireland the County Cavan and Galway names of Tully or McAtilla were frequently anglicised to Flood. They acted as hereditary physicians to both the O'Reillys and O'Connors.

Flynn (1) *Irish*. There were at least eight septs of this name, derived from the gaelic personal name Flann. There were two main concentrations of the name; in the Cork/Waterford area and in Roscommon, Leitrim and Cavan. The Northern sept of the name became known as Lynn. See Lynn.

Foley (3) *Irish.* This sept originated in County Waterford and from there spread into Counties Cork and Kerry. In parts of Ulster the County Leitrim sept of McSharry was anglicised to Foley.

Forbes (10) *Scottish.* This clan traces its descent from one John of Forbes who held the lands of Forbes in Aberdeenshire in the 13th century.

Ford (2) *Irish.* A number of septs, including the McKinnawes of Leitrim, anglicised their name to Ford. *English* and *Scottish.* Derived from a local name for someone who lived by a ford. A Devonshire family of this name settled in County Meath in the 14th century.

Forder (1) *English.* Meaning dweller at the ford there were places of this name in Devon and Cornwall. Forder is chiefly an East Anglian surname.

Forester (1) *English* and *Scottish.* Derived from the occupational name for a forest keeper it was first recorded as a surname in Scotland in the 12th century. At a later date it was often abbreviated to Foster. See Foster.

Forrester (1) See Forester.

Foster (14) *English* and *Scottish.* The most likely origin of this surname is as an abbreviated form of Forester (See Forester). The Fosters were one of the great riding clans of the Scottish Borders.

Fox (14) *Irish.* A number of distinct septs, including the McAtinneys (See Tinney) of Tyrone, anglicised their name to Fox. *English* and *Scottish.* Derived from a nickname referring to 'slyness'.

Foy (5) *Irish.* This sept which originated in County Fermanagh can trace its descent from Eoghan, son of the 5th century Niall of the Nine Hostages. They were hereditary tenants of the church lands of Derrybrusk in Fermanagh.

Frame (1) *Scottish.* Of uncertain derivation this surname was recorded in Lanarkshire from the late 15th century.

Francis (6) *English* and *Scottish.* Meaning a Frenchman, this popular Norman name of the Middle Ages was originally used in England to denote someone who was not an Anglo-Saxon. The surname was introduced at an early date to Scotland where it was recorded in Glasgow from the late 12th century.

Frank (1) *English* and *Scottish.* Derived from Norman Franc which was originally the name for the Germanic peoples who inhabited the lands around the River Rhine in Roman times. Families of this name became substantial landlords in Counties Leix and Offaly in the 17th century.

Fraser (2) See Frazer.

Frawley (1) A known variant of Farrell. See Farrell.

Frazer (10) *Scottish.* Derived from the place name of La Fresiliere in Anjou in France this surname was first recorded in Scotland in the 12th century. As Clan Fraser they acquired the lands of Lovat which stretched along the eastern shores of Loch Ness.

Frew (1) *Scottish.* This Perthshire surname was derived from the lands on the River Forth known as the Fords of Frew. In the Middle Ages this place held strategic importance as the lowest crossing point on the River Forth.

Friel (26) *Irish.* This County Donegal sept can trace their lineage to Eoghan, a brother of St. Columkille who founded the monastic settlement at Derry in 546. The Friels held the hereditary right of inaugurating O'Donnell as Lord of Tirconnell.

Fryer (2) *English.* This variant of Freer derived as a nickname for a 'religious person'. At the Reformation of the 16th century many friars renounced their vows, married and adopted the surname Frier.

Fullam (1) *English.* Derived from the place name of Fulham in Greater London it was recorded as a surname in Dublin in the 13th century.

Fullerton (3) *Scottish.* Derived from the lands of Fullerton in Ayrshire, meaning hamlet of the fowler, the Fullertons were a branch of Clan Stewart of Bute.

Fulton (7) *Scottish.* Derived from place names in Ayrshire and Roxburghshire, meaning muddy place it was first recorded as a surname in Paisley in 1260. Many Fultons from Ayrshire in particular settled in Ulster from the 17th century.

Funston (3) Outside Northern Ireland this name occurs only once in the telephone directories of Eire. In Northern Ireland there are 24 entries of the name, of which 16 of these occur west of the River Bann. The name originated in *Scotland* where it was perhaps a variant of Finnieston which was derived from a place name which is now part of the city of Glasgow.

Furey (1) *Irish.* Originating in County Westmeath this sept had by the end of the 16th century crossed the Shannon and settled in East Galway.

Furness (1) *English.* Derived from the name of the southermost point of the Furness peninsula in Lancashire.

G

Gabbie (1) A fairly common name in Northern Ireland, also spelt Gabbey, of uncertain origin. In 1890 of the five Gabbie births recorded in all of Ireland three were in County Down and the other two in Antrim.

Gailey (1) *Scottish.* A Northern Irish variant of gaelic Gallie, meaning stranger, which in the Highlands of Scotland was applied to people from the English-speaking Lowlands or of Norse origin.

Galbraith (12) *Scots Gaelic.* Meaning foreign Briton this name referred originally to the early Britons of Strathclyde who settled among the earlier Celtic peoples. The Galbraiths were septs of Clans Donald and MacFarlane.

Gallacher (1) See Gallagher.

Gallagher (170) *Irish.* This is the 3rd most common name in Derry. This County Donegal sept can trace its lineage to Conall Gulban, son of the 5th century Niall of the Nine Hostages. Controlling extensive territories stretching from Raphoe to Ballyshannon they were the chief marshalls in the army of the O'Donnell, Prince of Tirconnell.

Gallaugher (1) See Gallagher.

Gallick (5) Originating in *Italy* this surname is derived from latin Gallus which meant Gaul i.e. the early Celtic peoples of Western Europe.

Gamble (10) *English.* This name which frequently appeared in the

11th century Domesday Book was derived from an Old Norse personal name.

Garfiner (3) *English* and *Scottish.* Derived from the occupational name for someone who cultivated vegetables or fruit it was recorded as a surname in Scotland from the early 14th century.

Garfield (1) *English.* Derived from a place name, which can no longer be identified, referring to the triangular area left at the corner of a medieval open field after rectangular furlongs had been laid out.

Garland (1) *English* and *Scottish.* Derived either as an occupational name for a maker of garlands or as a local name meaning triangular peice of land (See Garfield). In Ireland Garnon, derived from the Norman nickname for someone who had a moustache, was changed to Garland (See Garnon).

Garnham (3) *English.* Derived from a place name, which can no longer be identified, meaning Gara's homestead, this surname is associated with Suffolk and Essex.

Garnon (4) *English.* Derived from an Old French nickname for someone who had a moustache this name came to Ireland with the Anglo-Normans in the 12th century. The name was frequently changed to Garland (See Garland).

Garvin (1) *Irish.* This sept which settled in County Mayo traces its descent from the 5th century Niall of the Nine Hostages.

Gault (5) *English* and *Scottish.* In England Gault is a variant of Galt which derived as a nickname from the wild boar while in Scotland it was a variant of Gall, meaning a stranger or a Lowlander (See Gailey).

Gavigan (2) *Irish.* This is a recorded variant of McGuigan (See McGuigan) and of Geoghegan, a County Westmeath sept which traces its descent from the 5th century Niall of the Nine Hostages.

Gavin (2) *Irish.* There were two septs of this name; one originating in County Mayo and the other in Southwest Cork. Gavin was also an Old Welsh personal name which became popular in England in the Middle Ages.

Geach (1) *English.* Derived as a nickname for a 'foolish person' this surname is associated with Devon and Cornwall.

Geary (1) *Irish.* Derived either from the County Cork sept name of

O'Geary or as a variant, found in Counties Armagh and Tyrone, of the Connaught sept name of McGarry .

Gee (1) *English.* A common name in Northern England of uncertain origin.

Gemelke (1) Originating from the State of Colorado, *U.S.A.* the bearer of this name came to Derry in 1967 to serve at the U.S. Naval Base at Clooney.

Gent (1) This is a recorded variant of the English names Gaunt and Gentle.

George (2) *English* and *Scottish.* Derived from a Germanic personal name which was in use in England before the Norman conquest. Found mainly in Ulster from the 17th century where Georges were mostly of Scottish origin.

Giacomin (1) This Italian variant of the Latin name Jacobus which was anglicised to both Jacob and James originated in the Veneto region in the Italian Alps to the north of Venice.

Gibbons (11) *Irish.* The Norman name of Fitzgibbon (See Fitzgibbon) and the County Mayo sept name of McGibbon, who were a branch of the Burkes, have been made Gibbons. *English.* Derived from a Germanic personal name.

Gibboney (1) *Irish.* A variant of Gibney which was the name of an ancient Irish sept. This name is fairly common in Counties Cavan and Meath.

Gibson (15) *Scottish.* Stemming from the personal name Gilbert there were septs of this name attached to Clans Cameron, Campbell and Buchanan.

Giff (2) *Irish.* A variant of the North Connaught sept of McGuff which was also recorded as McGiff.

Gilchrist (2) *Irish* and *Scots Gaelic.* Meaning son of the servant of Christ septs of this name originated in North Connaught and County Longford. In Ulster Gilchrist is usually of Scottish origin where septs of this name belonged to Clans MacLachlan and Ogilvie.

Gildea (2) *Irish.* Meaning son of the servant of God this sept which originated in County Donegal were followers of the O'Donnells. The name was also recorded as Kildea.

Gilfillan (6) *Scots Gaelic.* Meaning son of the servant of Fillan this name was futher anglicised to Gilliland (See Gilliland) and McLellan (See McClelland).

Gill (14) A variant of McGill. See McGill.

Gillard (2) *English.* A variant of the medieval given name Giles which was introduced to England by the Normans.

Gillen (13) *Irish.* A County Derry sept which can trace its lineage to Eoghan, son of the 5th century Niall of the Nine Hostages. Gillen, in many cases, has become indistinguishable from McGilligan. See McGilligan.

Gillespie (41) *Irish* and *Scots Gaelic.* This name originally meant son of the servant of the Bishop. In Ireland Gillespie originated as a County Down sept which settled, at an early period, in County Donegal where they became hereditary tenants of the church lands of Kilcar. In Scotland the Gillespies were a sept of Clan MacPherson. By translation the name also became Bishop. See Bishop.

Gillhan (1) See Gillen.

Gilliland (8) A variant of McClelland. See McClelland.

Gilloway (2) A variant of McElwee. See McElwee.

Gilmartin (1) *Irish.* Meaning son of the servant of Martin this County Tyrone sept was a branch of the O'Neills. Those members who moved south to Connaught became Kilmartin.

Gilmore (3) *Irish* and *Scots Gaelic.* This name originally meant son of the devotee of Mary. In Ireland the Gilmores were a County Down sept who traditionally followed the O'Neills of Clandeboy. In Scotland they were a sept of Clan Morrison in the Outer Herbrides.

Gilmour (5) See Gilmore.

Given (6) *Irish.* Formerly spelt Giveen this County Donegal sept was particularly associated with the Glenties area.

Glacken (1) This sept name is particularly associated with County Donegal.

Glackin (3) See Glacken.

Glasgow (2) *Scottish.* Derived from the old burgh of Glasgow it was first recorded as a surname in St. Andrews in the mid-13th century. *Irish.* In County Tyrone, in particular, Glasgow was frequently recorded as a variant of McCloskey. See McCloskey.

Glass (2) Can be of *English, Scottish* or *Irish* origin. In England it derived as an occupational name for a glazier or glass blower while in Ireland and Scotland it originated as an anglicised form of various gaelic surnames derived from the word glas which meant green. Glass is particularly associated with Counties Antrim and Derry.

Glavin (1) *Irish*. Originating in Connaught as O'Glavin this name is now rarely found outside Counties Cork and Kerry.

Glenn (21) *Irish* or *Scots Gaelic*. Derived from various local names referring to someone who lived in a valley. In Scotland the name was also derived from the lands of Glen in Peeblesshire.

Glover (1) *English* and *Scottish*. Derived from an occupational name for a maker or seller of gloves this surname was first recorded in Ireland in medieval times. The 17th plantation made the name quite common in Ulster.

Goan (2) An Ulster form of McGowan (See McGowan) which was often changed to Smith (See Smith).

Godfrey (8) *English* and *Scottish*. Derived from a Norman personal name which was, at an early date, borrowed by the Gaels of Ireland and Scotland to form McGorry and McCorry.

Golden (1) *Irish*. This is a recorded variant of McGoldrick (See McGoldrick). Furthermore a County Cork sept anglicised its name to Golden. *English*. Derived as a nickname for someone with golden hair.

Goligher (5) A variant of Gallagher. See Gallagher.

Goodall (1) *English* and *Scottish*. Derived either from the Yorkshire place name, meaning marigold nook or as an occupational name for a brewer or innkeeper it was recorded in Dublin from the 16th century.

Goodman (4) *Irish*. It is a recorded variant of McGuigan. See McGuigan. *English*. Derived either as an Old English personal name or as an occupational name for the master of a household.

Gordon (6) *Scottish*. A Norman family of this name settled in Berwickshire in the 12th century. On acquiring lands in Aberdeenshire in the 14th century they became a very powerful clan whose chief was known as the "Cock of the North".

Gorman (11) *Irish.* Originating in County Leix near the town of Carlow this sept settled in West Clare and Monaghan at the time of the Norman invasion. The Gormans of County Clare were herediatry marshalls to the O'Briens.

Gormley (22) *Irish.* Tracing their descent from Eoghan, son ot the 5th century Niall of the Nine Hostages this sept settled in County Tyrone, to the east of Strabane, in the 14th century when they were pushed out of their homeland in Raphoe, County Donegal by the O'Donnells.

Gough (3) *English.* Derived as an occupational name for a smith this surname is common in East Anglia. *Welsh.* Derived as a nickname for a 'red-haired person'.

Gourley (8) *Irish.* This variant of the Counties Armagh/Down sept of McTurley, meaning son of Turlough, was particularly associated with Counties Antrim and Tyrone.

Grace (2) *English.* Derived either as a nickname for 'a charming person' or from the popular medieval female name Grace. An Anglo-Norman family of the name acquired lands in County Kilkenny around 1200.

Graffin (1) The bearer of this name came to Derry from County Antrim in the early 1970s. Of 21 references to the name in the Northern Ireland telephone directories 17 of them are found in County Antrim.

Graham (17) *Scottish.* A Norman family of this name, derived from the Lincolnshire place name of Grantham, settled in Scotland in the early 12th century and acquired lands in Midlothian. They also settled in the Scottish Borders where they became one of the most powerful riding clans. In some cases Gormley was anglicised to Graham (See Gormley).

Grant (26) *Scottish.* This clan claims descent from Kenneth MacAlpine, the 9th century King of Scotland. In the 13th century they appear as Sheriffs of Inverness and from then upto the 17th century they asserted considerable influence in the Northeast of Scotland.

Gray (6) *English* and *Scottish.* Derived either from the nickname for 'grey-haired' or from the place name of Gray in Normandy. A

Norman family of the name settled in Scotland in the 13th century. The Grays were septs of Clans Sutherland and Stewart of Atholl as well as being one of the smaller riding clans of the Scottish Borders. In some cases the County Cavan sept of Culreavy was anglicised to Gray.

Green (21) *Irish.* A number of distinct septs, including the County Derry sept of McGlashan, anglicised their name to Green. *English.* Derived from a local name for someone who lived near a village green.

Greene (2) See Green.

Greenway (1) *English.* Derived from a local name for someone who lived by a grassy path it has been recorded in Ireland since the mid-17th century.

Greenwood (2) *English.* Derived from a local name for someone who lived in a dense forest.

Greer (4) *Scots Gaelic.* A branch of Clan MacGregor who settled in Dumfriesshire in the 14th century took this name. Greer was, furthermore, one of the names adopted by Clan MacGregor (See McGregor) on their proscription in the 17th century.

Gregg (4) *Scots Gaelic.* This was one of the names adopted by Clan MacGregor on their proscription in the 17th century (See McGregor). In England Gregg derived from the popular Middle Ages given name of Gregory.

Grey (1) See Gray.

Gribbons (1) *Irish.* This Ulster name is derived either from the Armagh sept name of McGribben or the Armagh/Down sept name of O'Gribben.

Grier (1) See Greer.

Grieve (3) *English* and *Scottish.* Derived from the occupational name for a steward or bailiff. Many Grieves or Greaves in Ulster were originally Greer (See Greer). In the late 16th century a branch of the Dumfries Greers settled in Northumberland before coming over to County Tyrone in the mid-17th century where they adopted the surname Grieves.

Griffen (4) *English* and *Welsh.* Derived either as a nickname for a 'fierce person' or as a variant of the Welsh personal name Griffith.

In fact a Welsh family of Griffen did settle in Ireland soon after the 12th century Anglo-Norman invasion. *Irish.* Most Griffins in Ireland were originally O'Griffy who originated as a sept in Northwest Clare.

Griffin (7) See Griffen.

Griffith (3) *Welsh.* Most Griffiths in Ireland were Welsh in origin, derived from the Old Welsh personal name Griffith. Occasionally the County Clare sept of O'Griffy (See Griffen) was anglicised to Griffith.

Griffiths (5) See Griffith.

Grimes (3) *English.* Derived from the Old Norse personal name Grim. *Irish.* The Connaught name of Grehan and the County Tyrone name of Gormley were both corrupted to Grimes.

Grimsey (1) Recorded only in Derry in the Northern Ireland phone book it may be a variant of Grimes (See Grimes).

Griscome (1) *English.* Derived from a local name which probably meant Gris's narrow valley. Combe is a very common element in English place names.

Groom (1) *English.* Derived from an occupational name for a servant or shepherd this surname is common in East Anglia.

Grumbleton (1) *English.* Derived from a local name meaning Grimbald's settlement. Grimbald was originally a Norman personal name.

Grumley (3) A variant of Gormley. See Gormley.

Guckian (1) A variant of McGuigan. See McGuigan.

Gunn (1) *Scots Gaelic.* This clan with territory in Caithness and Sutherland claims descent from Olave the Black, Norse King of the Scottish Isles and the Isle of Man in the early 13th century.

Gurney (8) *English* and *Scottish.* Derived from the French place name of Gournai-en-Brai a family of this name settled in Roxburghshire, Scotland in the late 13th century.

Guthrie (2) *Scottish.* Derived from the lands of Guthrie in Angus. In Ireland the County Clare sept name of Lahiff was sometimes anglicised to Guthrie.

Guy (5) *English.* Derived either from a French personal name which was recorded as both Why and Guy or from an occupational name for a guide. Guy was recorded in Ulster from the early 17th century.

Gwilt (1) *Welsh.* Derived from a nickname meaning 'wild' this surname was particularly associated with the Shrewsbury/Shropshire area.

H

Hagan (3) A variant of O'Hagan. See O'Hagan.

Haire (2) A Northern Irish variant of O'Hare. See O'Hare.

Hale (2) *English* and *Scottish.* Derived from a local name for someone who lived in a nook or hollow it was recorded in Scotland from the late 13th century.

Halford (1) *English.* Derived from a number of place names meaning ford in a nook or narrow valley this surname is chiefly found in the Midlands.

Hall (6) *English* and *Scottish.* Derived from a local name for someone who lived by or worked in the "Hall" or manor house. The Halls were one of the riding clans of the Scottish Borders. The name was first recorded in Ireland in the 14th century.

Halley (1) Can be of *English, Scottish* or *Irish* origin. In Northern England and Scotland it derived from an unidentified place name meaning Hall in an enclosure (see Hall). In Ireland two distinct septs with origins in Counties Clare and Tipperary anglicised their name to Halley.

Halpenny (2) *Irish.* This variant of the County Monaghan sept name of Halpin was recorded from the 16th century. There was also a Halpin sept in County Limerick but they didn't anglicise their name to Halpenny.

Halus (1) Originating in Poland as Halujhkawhich this family emigrated to the U.S.A. in the 19th century. Seventy years ago the name was shortened to Halus and twenty five years ago a family of the name settled in Derry.

Hamill (9) *Irish.* This County Tyrone sept traces their descent from Eoghan, son of the 5th century Niall of the Nine Hostages. From the 12th century they were hereditary poets to the O'Hanlons. *Scottish.* Common in Ayrshire Hamill derived from the Norman family of de Hameville who settled in Dumfriesshire in the 13th century.

Hamilton (89) *Scottish.* Derived from the Yorkshire place name of Hambleton, meaning crooked hill this surname was introduced to Scotland in the 13th century by a Norman family from Leicestershire. In the 14th century the Hamiltons were granted the lands of Cadzow in Lanarkshire by Robert the Bruce. Hamilton is a name very much associated with the Scottish "undertakers" or landowners who were granted large estates in Counties Armagh, Fermanagh and Tyrone at the time of the 17th century plantation of Ulster.

Hamm (1) *English.* Derived as a local name for someone who lived in a river meadow. *Scottish.* The Caithness surname of Ham was derived from a local place name meaning homestead.

Hampsey (2) *Irish.* The small County Derry sept of O'Hampsey or O'Hanson was usually recorded as Hampson by the 17th century. In England Hampson derived as a variant of the surname Hammond.

Hampson (2) See Hampsey.

Hancock (4) *English.* Meaning young Hann this surname was derived from the medieval given name of Hann which in turn was derived from the personal names of both John and Henry.

Hanlon (1) *Irish.* This sept were Lords of North and East Armagh and, together with the McGuinnesses, they controlled East Ulster.

Hanly (1) *English.* Derived from a number of place names, spelt as Handley or Hanley, meaning high clearing in a wood. *Irish.* The ancient Irish sept of Hanly originated on the banks of the Shannon in County Roscommon. A branch of this family later migrated to Cork.

Hanna (10) *Scots Gaelic.* A powerful sept in the Province of Galloway who were forced to submit to their Norman conquerors led by Edward Bruce in 1308.

Hannaway (4) *Irish.* A South Down variant of the County Down sept name of Hanvey.

Hannigan (5) *Irish.* This name which is particularly associated with Counties Tyrone and Waterford is of uncertain origin. It may be a variant of O'Hannon. (See Hannon)

Hannon (1) *Irish.* This sept originated in County Limerick although the Southeast Galway sept name of Haneen was frequently changed to Hannon.

Hansen (1) See Hampsey.

Harding (1) *English.* Derived from an old English personal name meaning brave or strong families of this name settled in Tipperary in the 17th century.

Hardy (1) Can be of *English, Scottish* or *Irish* origin. In England and Lowland Scotland it derived as a nickname for 'a brave man'. In the Highlands of Scotland the McHardys of Aberdeenshire became Hardy while in Ireland the now obsolete County Roscommon sept name of McGilledogher was anglicised to Hardy.

Hargan (15) *Irish.* This variant of the County Cork sept name of Horgan is largely confined to Ulster.

Harkan (1) See Harkin.

Harkens (1) See Harkin.

Harkin (114) *Irish.* This County Donegal sept, with their homeland in the Inishowen peninsula, were hereditary tenants of the church lands of Clonca, near Malin Head.

Harkness (3) *Scottish.* Derived from an unidentified place name, meaning dweller at the headland this surname was very much associated with Dumfriesshire in the 16th century. A branch of the Dumfriesshire Harknesses settled in Ulster in the 17th century.

Harley (9) *Irish.* A variant of the County Donegal sept name of Harrily. *English.* Derived from place names in Shropshire and West Yorkshire, meaning hares' wood.

Harper (9) *Scots Gaelic.* Derived from an occupational name referring to a harp player. The harper was an hereditary office in the households of most clan chiefs. Anglicised to Harper the original form of the name was McWhirter. The Harpers or McWhirters were a sept of Clan Buchanan and the name was commonest in Argyllshire and Stirlingshire.

Harpur (1) See Harper.

Harrigan (29) *Irish.* As well as being a recorded variant of Horgan (See Hargan) there was a County Leix sept who anglicised their name to Harrigan.

Harrington (1) *English.* Derived from place names in Cumberland, Lincolnshire and Northamptonshire. *Irish.* The West Cork sept, whose name was recorded as O'Hungerdell in the 17th century, has now largely been anglicised to Harrington. The sept names of Heraghty in Galway and Harraughton in Kerry were sometimes anglicised to Harrington.

Harris (8) *English* and *Scottish*. Meaning son of Harry, this name was the English form of the popular Norman name Henry. In Scotland there was a Harris sept attached to Clan Campbell.

Harrison (9) See Harris.

Harron (4) See Herron.

Hart (3) Can be of *English, Scottish* or *Irish* origin. In Ireland a sept of O'Harts settled in County Sligo after being pushed out of their Meath homeland by the Norman invaders. In England Hart was derived from a nickname meaning 'deer' while in Scotland a family of the name acquired lands in Lanarkshire in the early 14th century and they took their name from the manor of Hert in Durham.

Harte (4) See Hart.

Hartin (3) *Irish*. This sept originated in County Longford. In a few cases Hartin may be confused with English Harton which was derived from place names found in Durham and North Yorkshire.

Hartop (1) *English*. It may be derived from a local name meaning grey hill.

Harvey (19) Can be of *English, Scottish* or *Irish* origin. In Ireland the County Donegal sept name of Harrihy was anglicised to Harvey. In England and Scotland the name was derived from an Old French name, meaning battle worthy, which was introduced to Britain with the Norman invaders in the 11th century.

Haslam (1) *English*. Derived either as a local name for someone who lived by the hazel trees or from a Lancashire place name. It was recorded in Counties Leix and Offaly from the mid-17th century.

Haslett (8) *English*. Derived from a local name for someone who lived by a hazel copse. Although originally an English name Haslett and its variants such as Hazlett, Heslitt and Heazley are now chiefly found in Northern Ireland.

Hasson (23) *Irish*. Recorded as Hassan, Hassen, Hasson and Hessan this surname originated in County Derry.

Hastings (4) *English*. Derived from the place name in Sussex where William the Conqueror defeated King Harold in 1066. In Ireland the County Mayo sept of Hestin usually anglicised their name to Hastings.

Hatrick (2) *English* and *Scottish.* A variant of Arkwright which derived as an occupational name for a maker of chests. Hattrick and Hettrick are further spellings of this name.

Haverty (1) *Irish.* A variant of the County Galway sept name of Faherty.

Hawkins (2) *English.* Derived from the Old English personal name Hawk this surname occurs most frequently in the West Country and West Midlands. Irish Haughan was sometimes anglicised to Hawkins.

Hawthorne (5) *English* and *Scottish.* Derived either from the place name of Hawthorn in County Durham or from a local name for someone who lived near a hawthorn bush. In Scotland the name was established in Galloway at an early date and in Kintyre the Hawthorns were a sept of Clan Donald.

Hay (5) *English.* Derived either from a local name for someone who lived by an enclosure or as a nickname for a tall man. *Scottish.* Clan Hay trace their descent from William de la Haye who, through marriage, acquired the lands of Erroll in Angus in about 1160. Through their support for Robert the Bruce they received Slains castle in Aberdeenshire in the early 14th century.

Hayden (2) *Irish.* Also recorded as Headon and Heydon this sept originated in County Carlow. This name is now common in Tipperary. *English.* Derived either from Northumberland place names meaning hay valley or from place names in the Southern Counties meaning hay hill. A Norman family of this name settled in County Wexford in the late 12th century.

Hayes (3) *English.* Derived from a number of Southern English place names meaning either enclosures or brushwood. In County Wexford Hayes descend from a Norman family who settled there in 1182. *Irish.* There were at least 12 distinct septs whose names, meaning descendant of Hugh, were variously anglicised to O'Hea in Southwest Cork, Hughes in Ulster and Hayes in the remainder of the country.

Hayward (1) *English.* Derived from the occupational name for an official who was responsible for protecting land or forest from damage by animals or poachers.

Hazlett (5) See Haslett.

Healey (7) *Irish.* Two septs of this name originated independently in South Cork and on the western shore of Lough Arrow in County Sligo. In Cork the name was also known as Healihy.

Healion (1) *Irish.* A recorded variant of Phelan. (See Phelan)

Healy (13) See Healey

Heaney (21) *Irish.* The principal sept of this name were chiefs of Fermanagh before the Maguires took over in 1202. Another sept of the name were hereditary tenants of the church lands of Banagher in County Derry.

Heatherington (3) See Hetherington.

Heatley (7) *English* and *Scottish.* Derived from a number of place names, of which the most significant is in Cheshire, meaning heathy clearing. A family of this name held lands at Kelso in the Scottish Borders from the early 13th century.

Heavern (2) *Irish.* A variant of the County Mayo sept name of Heffron who trace their descent from Eoghan, son of the 5th century Niall of the Nine Hostages. A distinct sept of O'Heveran was established in County Antrim by the 17th century.

Hebden (1) *English.* Derived from the West Yorkshire place name meaning rose-hip valley.

Hedley (1) *English* and *Scottish.* Derived from a number of place names meaning a clearing overgrown with heather it was recorded in Scotland from the late 13th century.

Heenan (1) *Irish.* A small sept of this name was based in the Roscrea area on the North Tipperary/Offaly border. The name may also have originated in County Down.

Hegan (1) A variant of O'Hagan found in County Armagh. See O'Hagan.

Hegarty (72) *Irish.* Originating in South Derry this sept can trace its descent from Eoghan, son of the 5th century Niall of the Nine Hostages. By the 17th century they had established themselves in Inishowen, County Donegal and in County Derry, west of the River Roe. The Hegartys were sub-lords to the O'Neills.

Helferty (5) *Irish.* This Donegal name is also recorded as Hilferty, Halferty and Helverty.

Helliwell (1) *English* and *Scottish.* Derived from a great number of place names, meaning holy well, which were found throughout England and which are variously recorded as Holwell, Holywell, Halwill and Halwell. The surname was recorded in the Scottish Borders from the 15th century.

Henderson (21) *Scottish.* Derived from the popular Norman forename Henry the Hendersons were variously a sept of Clan Gunn in Caithness; a clan, with 8th century origins, in Glencoe in Argyllshire who in the 14th century became the bodyguards and hereditary pipers to the McDonalds of Glencoe; and one of the lesser riding clans of the Scottish Borders. (See also Henry)

Hendrix (1) A *Flemish* variant of Henry (See Henry). In Ireland the County Waterford sept of Hendrick were a branch of the McMurroughs.

Hennigan (1) *Irish.* A variant of the County Mayo sept name of Henaghan which was widely changed to Bird.

Henry (15) Can be of *English, Scottish* or *Irish* origin. In England it derived from the Germanic personal name Henry which was introduced there by the Normans. In Scotland the Henrys of Argyll and Bute were originally McKendricks (See McKendrick). In Ireland the North Antrim/Derry sept of McHenry, who were a branch of the O'Kanes, and the County Derry sept of O'Henery were further anglicised to Henry.

Hepburn (6) *Northern English* and *Scottish.* Derived from the Northumberland place name meaning high burial mound. At an early date the Hepburns acquired lands in East Lothian, Scotland.

Heraghty (1) *Irish.* Mainly associated with Counties Donegal, Galway and Mayo it is often a variant of Geraghty. Based in Counties Roscommon and Galway the Geraghtys were sub-lords to the O'Connors.

Heron (1) See Herron.

Herrick (1) *Irish.* A variant of the County Tyrone name of Ercke. This sept claims descent from Erc, the eldest son of Colla Uais, the 4th century semi-ledgendary King of Ireland. In England Herrick derived from the Old Norse personal name of Eric.

Herrity (1) A variant of Heraghty. (See Heraghty)

Herron (13) *Irish.* Two septs, one originating in County Armagh and the other in Donegal, anglicised their names to Harran, Herron or Heran. The County Armagh sept name of McElheron, meaning son of the devotee of Ciaran, was in some cases shortened to Heron. *Scottish.* On the Isle of Bute there was a sept of McElheran attached to Clan Donald while in the Scottish Borders the Herons were one of the lesser riding clans. In England Heron derived as a nickname for a thin man with long legs.

Hetherington (17) *English.* Derived from a Northumberland place name meaning settlement of the dwellers on the heath. The name was established in County Leix in the 16th century although it is now mainly found in County Tyrone.

Heverin (1) See Heavern.

Hewitt (3) *English* and *Scottish.* Usually meaning little Hugh this name also derived as a local name for someone who lived in a clearing in a forest. In Scotland the surname became common in Berwickshire.

Hickey (5) *Irish.* As hereditary physicians to the O'Briens this sept originated in County Clare and North Tipperary.

Higgenbotham (1) *English.* Derived from the Lancashire place name, originally known as Akenbottom, meaning broad valley with oak trees.

Higgins (12) *Irish.* Claiming descent from Niall of the Nine Hostages this sept originated in the Midlands of Ireland but spread westward into Mayo and Sligo. Some will be of English descent where the name origianlly meant little Richard.

Hill (5) *English* and *Scottish.* Derived from a local name for someone who lived near a hill it was recorded as a surname in Scotland from the late 13th century. In Northwest Ulster some Boyles may have adopted the name Hill (see Boyle).

Hillen (5) *Irish.* A recorded variant of Phelan. See Phelan. *English.* A rather rare surname which originated in Essex and Suffolk.

Hillick (1) *Scottish.* Derived from a local name for someone who lived by a hill this surname was recorded in Glasgow in the early 16th century.

Hinds (6) *Irish.* The South Galway sept of O'Heyne and the County Fermanagh sept of O'Keown (See Owens) anglicised their name to Hinds and Hynes. *English.* Derived either from an occupational name for a servant or as a nickname for a gentle or timid person.

Hippsley (1) *English.* Derived from the place name of Ipsley in Warwickshire meaning wood on the hill.

Hiscox (3) *English.* Meaning little Richard this name is mainly associated with the Dorset, Wiltshire and Somerset area.

Ho (2) There are 6 listings of this Chinese name in the telephone directories of Eire. In Northern Ireland the only reference to Ho is in Derry.

Hockley (2) *English.* Derived from a number of place names meaning Hocca's wood or hill.

Hodge (1) *English.* This medieval given name was derived from the personal name Roger. In some cases Hodge originated as a nickname for a person who supposedly resembled a hog or a pig.

Hogan (2) *Irish.* There were three distinct septs of this name, with the major one originating in County Clare as a branch of the O'Briens. Today most Hogans live in Counties Clare, Limerick and Tipperary.

Hogg (9) *English* and *Scottish.* Derived as a nickname from the animal i.e. hog or pig. In Ireland Hogg may, in some cases, be a variant of O'Hagan (See O'Hagan).

Holahan (1) *Irish.* A variant of Hoolahan with prominent septs of this name originating in Counties Clare and Kilkenny.

Holcomb (1) *English.* Derived from various place names meaning deep valley.

Holden (4) *English.* Derived from place names in Lancashire and West Yorkshire meaning deep valley. At the end of the 12th century a Welsh family known as Howlin, whose name later became Holden, settled in Counties Kilkenny and Wexford.

Holland (1) Can be of *English, Scottish* or *Irish* origin. In England it was derived from a number of place names meaning ridge land and it was first recorded as a surname in Scotland in the mid-15th century. In Ireland Holland can be an abbreviation of Mulholland

(See Mulholland) or a variant of Hoolahan (See Holahan).

Hollingsworth (1) *English.* Derived from place names in Cheshire and Lancashire meaning holly enclosure it was recorded in Connaught in the mid-17th century.

Hollington (1) *English.* Derived from various place names meaning holly settlement.

Hollins (1) *English.* Derived from a local name, chiefly found in Yorkshire, for someone who lived by a group of holly trees.

Holloway (1) *English.* Derived from a number of place names meaning sunken path.

Holly (2) A variant of Hollins. See Hollins.

Holmes (13) *Scots Gaelic.* A number of septs, whose name meant son of Thomas, anglicised their name to Holmes and to McComb (See McCombe). Septs of this name were attached to Clans Campbell, Mackintosh, MacThomas and MacTavish. Some may take their name from the lands of Holmes in Ayrshire. *English.* Derived from a local name for someone who lived on fen land.

Hone (3) *Irish.* In the 17th century a sept name of O'Hone was recorded in County Monaghan. Furthermore a Dutch family of this name settled in Ireland. *English.* Derived from a local name for someone who lived by a boundary stone.

Hood (1) Can be of *English*, *Scottish* or *Irish* origin. In England it derived either as an occupational name for a maker of hoods or as a nickname for someone who wore a distinctive hood. The name was recorded at an early date in Scotland while in Ireland a sept known as Hood or Mahood were hereditary bards of the O'Neills of Clandeboy. They were chiefly located in Counties Antrim and Down.

Hooper (1) *English.* Derived as an occupational name for someone who fitted hoops on wooden barrels.

Hooton (1) A variant of Hutton. See Hutton.

Horner (4) *English* and *Scottish.* Derived as an occupational name for a maker of horn objects. It is chiefly a Yorkshire surname although it was recorded in Arbroath, Scotland in the mid-15th century.

Horshi (1) This name is *Iranian* in origin.

Horton (3) *English.* Derived from numerous place names meaning mud settlement.

Horwill (1) *English.* Derived from a Devonshire place name meaning mud spring.

Houghton (1) *English.* Derived from a number of place names meaning ridge settlement. *Irish* A number of septs such as Haughan and O'Haghtir of North Tipperary anglicised their name to Houghton.

House (2) *English.* Derived from a local name for someone who was associated with the largest building, such as a church or manor house, in a medieval settlement.

Houston (18) *Scottish.* Meaning Hugh's place many Houstons descend from a Norman family which settled in Lanarkshire in the 12th century. Their lands came to be called Huston and, at a later date, they adopted their estate's name as their surname. In some cases in Donegal McHugh was anglicised to Huston (See McHugh).

Houton (1) A variant of Hutton. See Hutton.

Howard (1) *English.* Derived from both a Norman and Scandinavian personal name. *Irish.* The County Clare sept of O'Hure anglicised their name to Howard.

Howe (1) *English.* Derived from a local name for someone who lived by a small hill. *Irish.* Hoey (See Huey) and the County Clare sept name of Haugh were sometimes anglicised to Howe.

Howie (3) *Northern English* and *Scottish.* Derived either from the personal name Hugh or from a now unknown place name in Ayrshire this surname was recorded in Scotland from the early 16th century.

Hoy (1) *Irish.* The sept name of Haughey, with origins in Counties Armagh and Donegal, was sometimes anglicised to Hoy. *Scottish.* Derived either from the island of Hoy in Orkney or from a place of the name in the Scottish Borders.

Hoyle (2) Can be of *English*, *Scottish* or *Irish* origin. In England and Scotland it derived as a local name for someone who lived by a hollow. In Ireland Hoyle can be a variant of McIlholye which was normally anglicised to Coyle (See Coyle).

Hubbard (1) *English.* Derived from the Germanic personal name Hubert which was introduced to England by the Normans.

Huey (7) *Northern English* and *Scottish.* Derived from the personal name Hugh. *Irish.* A variant of Hoey who were an important sept in County Down until they were subdued by the Dunlevys around 1300.

Hughes (12) *English.* Meaning son of Hugh this popular personal name was introduced to Britain by the Normans in the 11th century. *Irish.* At least five septs in Ulster whose names meant descendant of Hugh anglicised their name to Hughes (See also Hayes). The Ulster septs of this name originated in West Armagh, South Donegal, South Down, South Monaghan and North Tyrone.

Hume (4) *English* and *Scottish.* Derived from local names for someone who lived either by a holly tree or on an island. In addition in Scotland the name was derived from the lands of Home in Renfrewshire. In Ireland the surname is particularly associated with Antrim and Fermanagh.

Humphreys (1) *English* and *Scottish.* Derived from the Old French personal name Humfrey which was introduced to Britain by the Normans.

Hunniford (1) *English.* Derived from a local name for someone who lived by a river ford where honey could be found.

Hunter (15) *English* and *Scottish.* Derived from an occupational name for a huntsman. It was first introduced to Scotland in the early 12th century by the Normans and the name became very common in Ayrshire. The Hunters were also one of the lesser riding clans of the Scottish Borders.

Hurley (1) *Irish.* Two septs, one originating in County Clare and the other in County Cork, anglicised their name to Hurley. In England Hurley derived from place names in Berkshire and Warwickshire meaning corner wood.

Hussey (2) *Irish.* This sept, with origins on the border of Counties Fermanagh and Tyrone, were hereditary bards to the Maguires. In Counties Kerry and Meath Hussey was a variant of de Hosey which was derived from a French place name and introduced to Ireland by an Anglo-Norman family.

Huston (1) See Houston.

Hutahean (1) See Hutchinson.

Hutcheon (2) See Hutchinson.

Hutcheson (2) See Hutchinson.

Hutchinson (9) *Scots Gaelic*. Meaning son of Hutcheon, which in turn meant little Hugh, this sept with origins in the Isle of Skye trace their descent from Hugh son of Alexander MacDonald, Lord of the Isles.

Hutchison (1) See Hutchinson.

Hutchman (6) See Hutchinson.

Hutton (22) *English* and *Scottish.* Derived from a great number of place names meaning ridge settlement it was recorded as a surname in Scotland in Lanarkshire from the mid-13th century.

Hyland (1) *Irish.* A variant of Phelan. See Phelan. *English.* Derived from a local name for someone who lived on high ground.

Hyndman (11) *English* and *Scottish.* Derived from an occupational name for a servant this surname is now chiefly found in Northern Ireland. Hyndman was recorded in Renfrewshire, Scotland from the 16th century. (See also Hinds).

Hynds (1) See Hinds.

Hynes (3) See Hinds.

I

Inglis (1) A variant of English. See English.

Irvine (10) *Scottish.* Derived from the parish of Irving in Dumfriesshire the Irvines became one of the more troublesome riding clans of the Scottish Borders. During the plantation of Ulster many Irvines settled in Fermanagh where they gave their name to Irvinestown. The name has, however, become confused with Irwin (See Irwin).

Irwin (15) *Scottish.* Derived from the Old English personal name of Irwyn. During the 17th century plantation most Irwins who settled in Ulster came from Dumfriesshire. Although a distinct name Irwin is often confused with Irvine (See Irvine).

J

Jaber (1) In all of Ireland the only reference to Jaber in the telephone directories is in Derry.

Jack (2) *English* and *Scottish.* Derived from the personal names of either Jacob or John it was recorded as a surname in Scotland from the late 15th century. This surname is now common in Counties Donegal and Tyrone.

Jackaman (1) *English.* Derived as an occupational name for the servant to a man called Jack (See Jack).

Jackson (26) *English* and *Scottish.* Meaning son of Jack (See Jack) this surname is very common in all parts of the British Isles. In Ulster it is found mainly in Counties Antrim and Armagh.

Jagota (1) In all of Ireland the only reference to Jagota in the telephone directories is in Derry.

Jain (1) In this case Jain originated in India and the name first came to Derry in 1969. Jain is also an English name; a variant of Jane found in Devon and Cornwall.

James (3) Can be of *English, Scottish* or *Irish* origin. In England and Lowland Scotland it was derived ultimately from the Old Testament name of Jacob. Anglo-Norman Fitzjames and Irish and Highland Scottish McJames were abbreviated to James.

Jamieson (3) *Scottish.* The Jamiesons were variously a sept of Clan Gunn; a sept of Clan Stuart on the Isle of Bute and one of the smaller riding clans in the Scottish Borders.

Jamison (1) See Jamieson.

January (1) *English.* Derived from a nickname or given name for someone born in January.

Jarvis (6) *English.* Derived either from the Old French forename Gervase or from the North Yorkshire place name of Jervaulx it was first recorded in Ireland in the early 14th century.

Jefferson (3) This name means son of Jeffrey. See Jeffrey.

Jeffrey (3) *English* and *Scottish.* Derived from the Norman personal name Geffrey which gave rise to surnames such as Jeffrey, Jeffreys, Jeffers, Jefferson and Geoffrey. These surnames were particularly common in Aberdeen, Scotland. In Ireland Jeffries and Jefferson became McSheffrey (See McSheffrey).

Jeffreys (1) This name means son of Jeffrey. See Jeffrey.

Jenkins (2) *English.* Meaning son of Jenkin, which in turn meant young John, this name is thought to be Flemish in origin.

Jennings (6) *English.* This name literally means son of little John. *Irish.* Holding extensive lands in Galway and Mayo the Jennings were a branch of the Burkes.

Jessop (1) *English.* Derived from the biblical name Joseph, Jessop represents the usual pronounciation of the name in the Middle Ages.

Johnson (2) See Johnston.

Johnston (45) *Scottish.* Strictly speaking Johnson and Johnston are two distinct names; the former meaning son of John and the latter John's town. The two names, however, are now indistinguishable one from the other. The Johnstones were one of the great riding clans of the Scottish Borders who settled in Dumfriesshire in the lands of Johnstone in the 12th century. During the plantation of Ulster many of them settled in Fermanagh. Furthermore septs of Clan Gunn in Caithness and of Clan Donald in Glencoe anglicised their name to Johnson and Johnston. In Ireland a number of septs including McKeown (See McKeown) and McShane (See McShane) anglicised their name to both Johnson and Johnston.

Johnstone (5) See Johnston.

Jones (12) *Welsh.* Meaning son of John this extremely popular Welsh name is especially associated with Counties Antrim and Armagh where English settlement dominated during the plantation.

Jordan (5) *English.* Derived from the River Jordan in the Middle East. In the 12th century the Crusaders brought home water from the Jordan for baptismal purposes and popularised the personal name Jordan. The Anglo-Norman invaders of the late 12th century introduced the name to Ireland.

Joseph (2) See Jessop.

Joyce (2) *Welsh.* Derived from a Breton personal name this name was introduced to Ireland in the 12th century by Normans from Wales. Settling in Counties Galway and Mayo, as sub-lords to the O'Flahertys, the Joyces became regarded as a true gaelic sept.

K

Kam (1) Originating in Malaysia this surname came to Ireland in 1984.

Kane (15) See O'Kane.

Kavanagh (6) *Irish*. This sept, with origins in County Wexford, were of the same stock as the McMurroughs, the late 12th century kings of Leinster. The McCavanas of East Tyrone and the McKevenys of South Antrim sometimes anglicised their name to Kavanagh.

Kay (1) *English* and *Scottish*. This name has various origins including; an occupational name for a maker of keys; a local name for someone who lived by a wharf; and a Celtic personal name. In the Highlands of Scotland and the Isle of Man Kay was recorded as a shortened form of Mackay from the 17th century (See McCay).

Kayne (4) As well as being a variant of O'Kane (See O'Kane) Kayne originated in England as a nickname for a tall, thin man.

Kealey (2) *Irish*. Kealey can be variants of the County Limerick sept name or Kiely, the County Galway sept name of Keeley, the County Kilkenny and North Clare sept names of Queally and even of Kelly (See Kelly).

Keanie (1) *Irish*. This surname seems to have originated in two areas; Leitrim and Southwest Donegal and in Wexford and Carlow. To some extent the name has been absorbed into Kenny in County Leitrim and McKenna in Wexford.

Kearney (16) *Irish*. Tracing their descent from Eoghan, son of the 5th century Niall of the Nine Hostages the Kearneys were a branch of the O'Hanlons of Armagh.

Kearns (2) *Irish*. This variant of the County Mayo sept name of O'Kieran is common in Fermanagh and Monaghan. The name has become confused with Cairns (See Cairns) and in Donegal there are instances where the name was changed to Kerr (See Kerr).

Keaveney (2) *Irish*. This sept which originated in County Galway also anglicised its name to Geaveney. In some cases the name was changed to the better known Kavanagh (See Kavanagh).

Keddy (2) *Scottish.* A variant of McAdie which was derived from the personal name Adam. The McAdies were septs of Clans Gordon and Ferguson.

Kee (5) See McKee.

Keegan (4) See McKeegan.

Keenan (20) *Irish.* A County Fermanagh sept who acted as historians to the Maguires and who were hereditary stewards of the church lands of Cleenish.

Keeney (1) See Keanie.

Kehoe (6) See Keogh.

Keith (1) *Scottish.* Through marriage this clan acquired lands in Caithness in the 14th century where they came into conflict with the already established Clan Gunn.

Kelleher (1) *Irish.* As a branch of the O'Briens this sept originated in County Clare. In the 14th century they migrated to Counties Cork and Kerry.

Kellock (2) As well as being a variant of Irish Kelly (See Kelly) Kellock was a variant of the Highland of Scotland sept name of MacKelly. It was also recorded as a surname in Aberdeenshire in the mid-14th century where it may have derived from the place name of Keiloch.

Kelly (142) *Irish.* At least seven distinct septs of the name established themselves in Ireland, the most powerful of which ruled over a territory which included East Galway and South Roscommon. In Ulster a Kelly sept, claiming descent from Colla the 4th century King of Ulster was based in South Derry. Kelly was known as a surname in Scotland long before 19th century immigration really established the name there; there was a Kelly sept attached to Clan Donald.

Kelpie (2) This name originated in *Scotland.* It may be a variant of Keltie which was derived from the lands of Keltie in Perthshire.

Kelso (1) *Scottish.* Derived from the town of Kelso in Roxburghshire, situated on the River Tweed, meaning chalk ridge.

Kemps (1) *English* and *Scottish.* Derived from an occupational name for a champion at jousting this surname is chiefly found in Southern England.

Kendall (1) *English.* Derived either from the place name Kendale in Yorkshire, meaning spring valley or from Kendal in Cumberland, meaning valley of the River Kent.

Kennedy (16) *Irish.* This sept takes its name from the father of Brian Boru, the early 11th century High King of Ireland. Originating in East Clare they later settled in North Tipperary where they became lords of Ormond from the 11th century to the 16th century. In the early 17th century a branch of the sept settled in County Antrim. *Scottish.* Originating in Ayrshire in the 12th century the Kennedys settled in Lochaber in Inverness-shire where they were a sept of Clan Cameron.

Kennelly (1) *Irish.* Recorded as a variant of both the West Cork sept name of Quinnelly and of the County Limerick sept name of Kinneally. In some instances Kennelly can be a variant of Connelly (See Connolly).

Kennerley (1) This may be a variant of Kennelly (See Kennelly).

Kenwell (3) *English.* Derived from the Suffolk place name of Kentwell meaning stream of the River Kent.

Keogh (5) *Irish.* Three distinct septs of this name originated in South Tipperary, South Roscommon and County Wicklow. The latter were hereditary poets to the O'Byrnes. This surname is also spelt Kehoe.

Kerlin (1) *Irish.* This variant of Carolan (See Carlin) is found in Counties Derry and Donegal.

Kerr (24) *Scottish.* As one of the great riding clans they settled in Roxburgh in the Scottish Borders in the 14th century. The majority of Ulster Kerrs are of this origin. Kerr, however, has become confused with Carr (See Carr).

Kerrigan (11) *Irish.* This sept originated in County Mayo. A branch later migrated to the Stranorlar area in County Donegal and, by the mid-17th century, the name was also well established in County Armagh.

Ketelaar (1) *Dutch.* Originating in the Province of Drente or Overijssen in Holland this name arrived in Derry in 1978.

Keys (34) *English* and *Scottish.* This name has various origins including: an occupational name for a key maker; a Welsh personal name i.e. Kay; and a local name for someone who lived near a quay. In Northern Ireland, however, most Keys will originally have been McKees (See McKee).

Khera (1) Originating from the State of Punjab in Northern India the bearer of this name came to Derry in 1943 to work with his cousin who was already settled here.

Kildea (1) See Gildea.

Kilgore (15) *Scottish.* Derived from the Fifeshire place name of Kilgour meaning goat wood this name was common in Fifeshire and Aberdeenshire. In Ireland the Northwest Ulster sept name of Kilgar was anglicised to Kilgore.

Kilkey (1) *Irish.* In Derry city, around 1900, Kilkey was recorded as a variant of Small (See Smalls).

Kilkie (2) See Kilkey.

Killen (7) A variant of McCallion. See McCallion.

Kilpatrick (1) *Scots Gaelic.* Derived from a number of place names meaning church of Patrick the Kilparticks were a sept of Clan Colquhoun.

Kincaid (5) *Scottish.* Derived from the lands of Kincaid in Stirlingshire this name was well established in Counties Antrim and Derry by the mid-17th century.

King (17) *English* and *Scottish.* As a nickname King was widely adopted as a surname in England and Scotland. In Perthshire a sept of Clan MacGregor anglicised their name to King. Some Ulster septs such as McAree of Monaghan and McGinn of Tyrone anglicised their name to King.

Kinkaid (2) See Kincaid.

Kinsella (1) *Irish.* This sept originated in County Wexford as a branch of the McMurroughs.

Kirby (2) *English.* Derived from a number of Northern English place names meaning chruch settlement. *Irish.* A County Limerick sept anglicised their name to Kirby and Kerwick while the County Mayo sept of Kerribly is now better known as Kirby.

Kirk (7) *Scottish.* Derived from a local name for someone who lived near a church. In County Derry especially Kirk has become indistinguishable from Kirkpatrick. The latter take their name from a church dedicated to St. Patrick in Dumfriesshire.

Kirkwood (3) *Scottish.* Derived from place names in Ayrshire, Dumfriesshire and Lanarkshire meaning wood belonging to the church or wood situated by the church.

Kitson (9) *Scots Gaelic.* An anglicisation of McCutcheon which is now better known as Hutchinson (See Hutchinson). *English.* First recorded in the 14th century this surname originally meant son of Christopher.

Kivlehan (3) *Irish.* Originating in County Westmeath this surname is now chiefly found in Counties Leitrim and Sligo.

Knight (1) *English* and *Scottish.* Derived from the status name Knight which, in the Middle Ages, denoted a man of substance who could maintain a horse and armour in order to serve his lord as a mounted soldier. It may in some cases be a shortened form of McKnight (See McKnight).

Knights (1) This variant of Knight was chiefly found in Norfolk.

Knox (7) *Scottish.* Derived from the lands of Knock in Renfrewshire. The family which adopted this name acquired these lands in the early 13th century. One branch of this family later settled at Prehen in Derry.

Kydd (3) *English* and *Scottish.* Derived from a nickname meaning 'kid' i.e. a young goat. In Scotland the name derived as a pet form of Christopher and it had long associations with Angus. The Kyd family played a prominent part in the affairs of Dundee from the mid-14th century.

Kyle (9) *Scottish.* Derived from the district of Kyle in Ayrshire this name came to Counties Antrim and Derry with the 17th century plantation of Ulster.

L

Lacey (2) *English.* Derived from the French place name of Lassy families of this name came to England with William the Conqueror. One of their descendants, Hugh de Lacy received the submission of Roderic, King of Connaught, on behalf of Henry II in 1172 and became 1st Lord of Meath. Lacys also established themselves in

County Limerick as well as in Meath. In addition a County Wexford sept anglicised their name to Lacy.

Lafferty (10) *Irish.* This County Donegal sept was also known by the name Laverty (See Laverty). Their chiefs were Lords of Aileach before they were driven from their homeland in the 13th century and settled near Ardstraw in County Tyrone.

Lagan (2) A variant of Logan. See Logan.

Laird (11) *Scottish.* Derived from the status name for a landlord this surname was recorded in Berwickshire from the mid-13th century.

Lambert (1) *English* and *Scottish.* Derived either from a Germanic personal name or from the occupational name for a shepherd. Lambarts from Preston established themselves in Ireland in the early 17th century as Earls of Cavan.

Lamberton (7) *Scottish.* Derived from the lands of Lamberton in Berwickshire it was recorded as a surname there from the 12th century.

Lampen (1) *English.* Derived from Lamb which originated either as a nickname for 'a meek person' or as an occupational name for a keeper of lambs.

Lamrock (2) *English* and *Scottish.* As Lamrick this surname had established itself in the Claudy area, County Derry by 1796. It perhaps originated as Lambrick which was derived from the Germanic personal name Lambert (See Lambert).

Langan (1) *Irish.* There were two distinct septs of this name; one originated in County Armagh but settled in Mayo while the other were hereditary stewards of church lands in County Limerick. This name has been further anglicised to Long (See Long).

Langman (1) *English.* Derived from a nickname for a 'tall person' (See Long).

Lanigan (1) *Irish.* This sept originated in County Kilkenny and North Tipperary.

Lappen (1) *Irish.* Originating in County Donegal this sept migrated to Armagh sometime after the 11th century. In the 10th century the Lappens were hereditary stewards of the church lands in Derry.

Lapsley (2) *Scottish.* This surname was recorded in both Stirling and Edinburgh in the mid-17th century.

Larmour (3) *English* and *Scottish.* Derived from an occupational name of Norman origin meaning armourer it was recorded as a surname in Scotland from the late 13th century.

Latimer (2) *English* and *Scottish.* Derived from the occupational name for a clerk or keeper of records in Latin. It was recorded as a surname in Yorkshire from the 13th century. In 1587 the Latimers were listed as one of the unruly clans of the Scottish Borders.

Latta (2) *Scottish.* Derived from the lands of Lawtie in Ayrshire it was first recorded as a surname in the late 17th century.

Laughland (1) See McLaughlin.

Laughlin (3) See McLaughlin.

Laverty (5) *Scots Gaelic.* A sept of Clan Donald who were hereditary heralds to the Lords of the Isles. Originating in Kintyre they were later based on Islay. Laverty can also be another form of Lafferty (See Lafferty).

Lavery (6) *Irish.* This sept, who took their name from their 11th century chief, originated in Moira, County Down. The Laverys formed into three branches known by the titles White, Red and Strong. The name was also anglicised to Lowry (See Lowry).

Lavy (2) *Irish.* A variant found in County Westmeath of the County Longford sept name of Leavy.

Lawrance (1) See Lawrence.

Lawrence (1) *English* and *Scottish.* Derived from the Old French given name of Laurence it was recorded as a surname in Lancashire from the early 14th century and in Aberdeen from the mid-16th century.

Leake (1) *English.* Derived either as a local name for someone who lived by a stream or as an occupational name for a grower or seller of leeks.

Leath (1) *Scottish.* Derived from the town of Leith in Midlothian it was first recorded as a surname in the mid-14th century.

Leathem (2) *Scottish.* Derived either from the manor of Letham in Berwickshire or from the lands of Letham in Angus it was first recorded as a surname in the late 13th century.

Leckey (3) *Scottish.* Derived from the lands of Leckie in Stirlingshire the Leckys were a branch of Clan MacGregor. Lecky was a common name in Dunbartonshire and Stirlingshire and by the mid-17th century the surname was well established in Counties Derry and Donegal.

Lecky (2) See Leckey.

Lee (6) Can be of *English, Scottish* or *Irish* origin. In England and Scotland it derived from a local name for someone who lived by a wood. In Ireland various septs anglicised their names to Lee such as the O'Lees of Galway, who were physicians to the O'Flahertys, and the McLees of Leix.

Lees (4) *English.* Derived from a local name for someone who lived by pasture land this surname is chiefly found in Lancashire and Staffordshire. This surname is generally regarded as distinct from Lee (See Lee). *Scots Gaelic.* In the Highlands Lees was a recorded variant of the sept name, meaning 'son of the servant of Jesus', which was usually anglicised to McAleese and McAlish.

Leeson (1) *English.* Meaning son of Lettice this surname is chiefly found in Northamptonshire and it was introduced to Ireland in the 17th century. In some cases the County Tipperary sept name of Gleeson became Leeson.

Leighton (1) *English.* Derived from a number of place names meaning leek settlement. One family, for example, adopted this surname from the manor of Leighton in Shropshire in the 12th century.

Leinster (2) Of uncertain origin this surname is found mainly in the east of the Province. It could possibly be an anglicisation of the Galway/Mayo name of Lynagh which meant Leinsterman. It may even be a variant of English Linter which derived as an occupational name for a flax dresser.

Leiper (2) *Scottish.* Derived from the occupational name for a basket maker it was recorded as a surname in Edinburgh in the late 12th century.

Leitch (5) This is the Scottish form of Leech which derived as an occupational name for a physician. It was recorded as a surname from the 14th century.

Lemogniam (1) In all of Ireland the only reference to Lemogniam in the telephone directories is in Derry.

Leonard (11) *Irish.* Various Ulster septs adopted this English personal name when anglicising their name such as McAlinion of Fermanagh and O'Lunney of Donegal (See Lunney).

Leopard (1) *English.* Derived as a nickname from the animal.

Lesley (2) See Leslie.

Leslie (6) *Scottish.* This clan takes its name from the lands of Leslie in Aberdeenshire which they acquired in the 12th century.

Lewers (1) *Scottish.* Derived from the lands of Leuchars in Fifeshire it was recorded as a surname in Kirkcudbrightshire in the early 17th century. It may also be derived from English Ewer which derived as an occupational name for a transporter of water.

Lewis (4) Can be of *English, Scottish* or *Welsh* origin. In England it derived from the Norman personal name Lowis while in Wales it derived from the Welsh personal name Llywelyn. In Scotland the name derived either from the island of Lewis or from the sept name McLewis or McCloy on Arran Island. (See McCloy).

Liddy (2) *Irish.* This County Clare sept strongly resisted English incursions in the Thomond wars of the 14th century. In County Cavan Liddy became Leddy.

Lilburn (1) *English* and *Scottish.* Derived from a village name in Northumberland meaning Lilla's stream it was recorded as a surname in Aberdeen, Scotland from the mid-15th century.

Lindsay (13) *Scottish.* This clan traces its descent from one Baldric de Lindsay, a Norman who held extensive lands in Angus in the 12th century. In Ulster Lynch (See Lynch) and Lynn (See Lynn) were in some cases further anglicised to Lindsay.

Linehan (1) *Irish.* Originating as a sept in County Roscommon this surname is found largely today in Counties Limerick and Tipperary.

Ling (1) *English.* Derived from the Norfolk place name of Lyng meaning hillside.

Linton (4) *English* and *Scottish.* Derived from a number of place names found all over England and the Scottish Borders which usually mean either lime tree or flax settlement.

Liston (1) *English* and *Scottish.* Derived from place names in Essex, West Lothian and Midlothian, meaning Lissa's settlement.

Litchfield (2) *English.* Derived from place names in Staffordshire and

Hampshire meaning cleared land within a grey wood and slope in open country respectively.

Little (6) Can be of *English, Scottish* or *Irish* origin. In England it derived as a nickname meaning 'small' and in Scotland the Littles were one of the riding clans of the Scottish Borders. In Ireland many members of the County Monaghan sept of Beggan anglicised their name to Little.

Livingstone (2) *Scottish.* Derived from the lands of Livingston in West Lothian the family granted these lands in the 12th century adopted it as their surname. In Argyll the McLeas, a sept of Clan Stewart of Appin, whose name meant son of the physician, anglicised their name to Livingstone.

Lland (4) *Welsh.* Derived from local names to describe countryside as opposed to a town and to identify someone who lived in a forest glade.

Lock (1) *English* and *Scottish.* Derived as an occupational name for a locksmith and as a local name for someone who lived near an enclosure. Lock can also be a variant of Lucas (See Luke).

Lockhart (1) *Scottish.* Derived from a Germanic personal name families of this name were settled in Ayrshire and Lanarkshire by the 12th century.

Logan (13) *Scottish.* This clan, also known as McLennan, trace their origins to one Logan who, in the 14th century, acquired lands in Ross and Cromarty. Logan was originally derived from several places of the name, especially in Ayrshire, meaning little hollow. A Norman family of the name settled in Carrickfergus in the 12th century. Furthermore the County Galway sept name of Lohan was sometimes anglicised to Logan.

Logue (40) *Irish.* A County Galway sept, whose name originally meant descendant of the devotee of Maodhog, who migrated at an early date to Derry and Donegal. The name is now rare outside these two counties. Mulvogue was another form of the anglicisation of this name. In Donegal Logue was in some cases changed to Molloy (See Molloy).

Lok (1) A variant of Lock (See Lock) which was recorded in Scotland in the 15th century.

Long (26) Can be of *English, Scottish* or *Irish* origin. In England and Scotland it derived as a nickname meaning 'tall' while in Ireland the County Armagh sept name of Longan was anglicised to Long.

Longworth (2) *English.* Derived from place names in Berkshire and Lancashire meaning long homestead.

Lorenc (2) A variant of Lawrence (See Lawrence) recorded in that part of Poland which came under German influence.

Lorimer (1) A variant of Larmour. See Larmour.

Louden (3) *Scottish.* Derived from the Ayrshire place name of Louden, meaning beacon hill. In Fife Louden derived as a variant of the Lowland regional name of Lothian.

Lough (2) *Scottish.* Derived as a variant of Loch, the Scottish term for a lake, it was recorded in Ulster from the early 17th century. It may in some cases be an abbreviation of the County Mayo and Meath sept names of Loughnane.

Loughery (3) See Loughrey.

Loughlin (4) See McLaughlin.

Loughrey (13) *Irish.* Mainly found in Ulster, and originally meaning descendant of the early riser, this surname has, in some instances, become confused with the ecclesiastical sept names of Early in County Cavan and Loughran in County Armagh.

Love (7) Can be of *English, Scottish* or *Irish* origin. In England and Lowland Scotland Love derived either from an Old English female personal name or from a nickname meaning 'she-wolf'. In the Scottish Highlands, especially in Kintyre, McKinnon (See McKinney) and McKinven were anglicised to Love. In Ireland McGrath (See McGrath) was sometimes anglicised to Love.

Lowry (3) *Irish.* A variant of Lavery. See Lavery. *Scottish.* Derived from Laurie, a variant of the personal name Lawrence (See Lawrence), it was a common name in Dumfriesshire.

Luke (1) *English* and *Scottish.* Derived from the Latin given name Lucas which was popularised in the Middle Ages by St. Luke the Evangelist. In Scotland the Lukes were an offshoot of the Lamonts (See McClements). Furthermore McLucas (See McLucas) was sometimes anglicised to Luke.

Lumb (1) *English.* Derived from place names in Lancashire and West

Yorkshire, meaning pool.

Lumsden (1) *Scottish.* Derived from the old manor of Lumsden in Berwickshire, meaning Lum's valley.

Lundy (1) *Scottish.* Derived from the Perthshire place name of Lundie, meaning marsh. Although the infamous Robert Lundy associated with the Siege of Derry was an Englishman. Lundy in this case was perhaps derived from Lund which was the local name for someone who lived in a grove.

Lunny (1) *Irish.* This County Donegal sept originated in the Raphoe area but later migrated to Tyrone and Fermanagh.

Lusby (4) *English.* Derived from the Lincolnshire place name meaning Lutr's village. Lutr was an Old Norse personal name. Presumably, therefore, Lusby was originally a Viking settlement.

Lusk (1) *Irish.* Derived from the village of Lusk in County Dublin this surname is now mainly found in Northeast Ulster. This surname also found its way to Lanarkshire and the Scottish Borders.

Lyle (4) *English* and *Scottish.* Derived from Norman Lisle, which originated as a local name for someone who lived on an island, Lyle was recorded at an early date in Scotland. Lyles came to Ulster from Southwest Scotland in the early 17th century and the name is now most numerous in Counties Antrim and Derry.

Lynch (96) *Irish.* Derived from the personal name meaning mariner there were several septs of this name including one based in North Antrim and Derry. In medieval Galway Lynchs of Anglo-Norman origin were all-powerful. In England Lynch derived as a local name for someone who lived by a hill.

Lynn (9) *Irish.* As the Ulster form of Flynn (See Flynn) this sept once ruled the territory to the east of Lough Neagh in South Antrim. *Scottish.* Lynn was also known in Ayrshire and Wigtownshire from the 13th century where it was derived from the Peeblesshire place name meaning pool.

Lynne (1) See Lynn.

Lynott (1) *Welsh.* Originally a Norman family from Wales the Lynotts established themselves in County Mayo in the 13th century but their power and influence declined from the 17th century onwards.

Lyons (3) Can be of *English, Scottish* or *Irish* origin. In England and

Scotland it derived either from the personal name Leon or from a nickname meaning 'Lion'. In Ireland several septs such as Lehane of County Cork and Lyne of County Kerry further anglicised their names to Lyons.

Lysaght (1) *Irish.* Originating in County Clare this sept was an offshoot of the O'Briens. The name is now most numerous in Clare and Limerick.

Lyster (1) *English.* Derived as an occupational name for a dyer this surname is common in Yorkshire. *Scots Gaelic.* Lister or Lyster are recorded abbreviations of MacAlister (See McAllister) and McLeister. The latter, whose name meant son of the arrow maker (See also Fletcher), were a sept of Clan MacGregror.

Lyttle (25) See Little.

Mc

McAdams (11) *Irish.* Two Ulster septs, namely McCaw of County Cavan and McCadden of County Armagh anglicised their names to McAdam. *Scots Gaelic.* First recorded in 1160 the McAdams were a sept of Clan MacGregor in Ayrshire.

McAlinden (1) *Irish.* Meaning son of the devotee of Fintan this sept was a branch of the Muldorys of County Armagh. In Armagh and Tyrone the name has been recorded as Linden and in Down as Lundy. (See Lundy)

McAlister (4) See McAllister.

McAllister (18) *Scots Gaelic.* Meaning son of Alasdair, the gaelic form of Alexander, this clan is the earliest offshoot of the great Clan Donald. Descended from Alasdair Mor, the younger son of Donald of the Isles, this clan's territory was principally in Kintyre. They came to Ulster as galloglasses (mercenary soldiers) to the McDonnells of Antrim.

McAloon (1) A variant of McLoone which is well known in Fermanagh. See McLoone.

McAnaney (7) *Irish.* Meaning son of the dean this County Monaghan sept were abbots of Clones monastery in the 14th century.

McAnea (1) A variant of McNee. See McNee.

McAnearney (1) *Irish.* An Ulster variant of the County Clare sept name of McInerney.

McAnee (5) A variant of McNee. See McNee.

McAnena (2) *Irish.* A variant of McEneany which was borne by two distinct septs which originated in Counties Monaghan and Roscommon.

McAnulla (1) A variant of McNally. See McNally.

McAnulty (1) A variant of McNulty. See McNulty.

McArthur (1) *Scots Gaelic.* Claiming to be the older branch of Clan Campbell the McArthur Clan acquired extensive territory in Argyll in the early 14th century for their support of Robert the Bruce.

Macartney (1) See McCartney.

McAteer (8) *Irish.* A County Armagh sept whose name, meaning son of the carpenter, has become confused with Scottish McIntyre as McAteer was frequently made McIntyre (See McIntyre). In Fermanagh McAteer was sometimes anglicised to Wright (See Wright).

McAuley (8) *Scots Gaelic.* There were two septs of this name; on Lewis in the Hebrides they were a sept of Clan MacLeod while in Dunbartonshire the McAuleys were a branch of Clan MacGregor. A branch of the latter sept accompanied the McDonnells to the Glens of Antrim in the early 16th century. *Irish.* A County Fermanagh sept who trace their descent from Donn Carrach Maguire, the first Maguire King of Fermanagh, who died in 1302.

McBain (2) *Scots Gaelic.* Originating in Lochaber in West Inverness-shire this clan settled at Kinchyle at the northern head of Loch Ness.

McBay (4) *Scots Gaelic.* Recorded as a surname in the mid-16th century McBay is usually regarded as a variant of MacBeth. Macbeth, who became King of Scotland in the 11th century, was the subject of a Shakespeare play.

McBernie (1) A variant of McBurney. See McBurney.

McBerth (1) A variant of McBeth. See McBay.

McBrearty (9) *Irish.* A County Donegal sept whose name means son of Murtagh. In Scotland the same name was usually anglicised to McCurdy (See McCurdy).

McBride (36) *Irish.* Meaning son of the devotee of Brigid this County Donegal sept, who were based at Gweedore, were hereditary tenants of the church lands of Raymunterdoney. *Scots Gaelic.* This sept of Clan Donald, who were based on Arran Island, trace their descent from Gillebride, father of Somerled, the 12th century Lord of Argyll.

McBrine (2) See Breen.

McBurney (1) *Scots Gaelic.* A Dumfriesshire sept whose name was derived from a Norse personal name. Many McBurneys anglicised their name to Burns (See Burns).

McBurnie (1) A variant of McBurney. See McBurney.

McCabe (1) *Scots Gaelic.* A branch of the MacLeods of Harris in the Hebrides who, in the 14th century, came to Cavan as galloglasses (mercenary soldiers) to the O'Reillys. They also served as galloglasses to the Maguires of Fermanagh and the McMahons of Monaghan.

McCafferty (52) *Irish.* Meaning son of the horse rider this sept originated in County Donegal as a branch of the O'Donnells. The name has become confused with McCaffrey (See McCaffrey).

McCaffrey (2) *Irish.* Meaning son of Godfrey, which was a Norse personal name, this sept was a branch of the Maguries of Fermanagh. They trace their descent from Donn Carrach Maguire, King of Fermanagh, who died in 1302. The name has become confused with McCafferty (See McCafferty).

McCahill (1) *Irish.* Found mainly in Counties Cavan and Donegal McCahill, in some cases, became McCall (See McCall).

McCahon (2) *Irish.* A variant of the County Antrim and North Derry name of McCaughan (See McGahan).

McCall (1) A variant of McCaul. See McCaul.

McCallaon (1) A variant of McCallion. See McCallion.

McCallion (64) *Scots Gaelic.* Meaning son of Colin the McCallions were the galloglasses (mercenary soldiers) of Clan Campbell of Argyll. In the 16th century they came to Donegal to fight for the O'Donnells.

McCallum (1) *Scots Gaelic.* Meaning son of the servant of Columba this clan held lands, granted to them by the Campbells, in Lorn, Argyllshire.

McCalmont (1) *Scots Gaelic.* A sept of Clan Buchanan. Introduced into Ulster in the 17th century the name is now mainly associated with County Antrim.

McCambridge (1) *Scots Gaelic.* Meaning son of Ambrose this name was associated with the Mull of Kintyre. In County Antrim, where the name is mainly found, McCambridge has become Cambridge. (See Cambridge).

McCampbell (1) *Scots Gaelic.* Based in Galloway the McCampbells were a branch of Clan Campbell (See Campbell). Some members of this sept did settle in County Down.

McCamphill (3) *Irish.* A variant of McCawell. This sept, which originated in Clogher, County Tyrone, trace their descent from Eoghan, son of the 5th century Niall of the Nine Hostages. McCawell was also anglicised to Campbell and McCall.

McCandless (10) *Irish.* This Ulster name, derived from the Old Irish personal name of Cuindless, was also recorded as McAndles and McCanliss.

McCann (19) *Irish.* This County Armagh sept were Lords of Clanbrassil on the sourthern shores of Lough Neagh. The McCanns have beem recorded there since 1155. Prior to this the O'Garveys ruled this territory.

McCanny (1) *Irish.* Well known in Counties Clare and Tyrone McCanny is now frequently shortened to Canny (See Canny).

McCarrick (2) *Irish.* This Ulster name, derived from the Old Irish personal name of Cu-Charraige, was recorded in Scotland from the early 16th century.

McCarroll (3) See Carroll.

McCarron (30) *Irish.* This County Donegal sept can trace their lineage to Eoghan, son of the 5th century Niall of the Nine Hostages. It is also possible that a sept of this name originated along the banks of the Foyle and later migrated to Monaghan.

McCarter (18) A variant of McArthur. See McArthur.

McCarthy (4) *Irish.* Originating in Counties Cork and Kerry the McCarthys trace their descent from Eoghan, son of the 3rd century King of Munster, Oilioll Olum. From the 13th century the McCarthys were the leading sept in South Munster in the ancient Kingdom of Desmond.

McCartie (1) A variant of McCarthy. See McCarthy.

McCartney (21) *Scots Gaelic*. Meaning son of Art this sept was a branch of Clan Mackintosh. The name was recorded in Ayrshire and Galloway from the early 16th century and in Northeast Ulster from the mid-17th century. It is believed that Scottish McCartneys were originally Irish McCartans (See Cartin).

McCaughey (4) *Irish*. Derived from an Old Irish personal name which was anglicised to Aghy this spelling of the name is associated with Tyrone. Other variants of the name include McAghy, McGahey (See McGahey) and McGaughey (See McGaughey).

McCaul (12) *Irish*. The County Tryone sept of McCawell (See McGirr) and the County Monaghan sept of McColla, who were a branch of the McMahons, anglicised their names to McCaul. *Scots Gaelic*. Meaning son of Cathal, and anglicised as McAll, McCall and McCaul, this name was common in Dumfriesshire and Ayrshire. The McCauls originated as branches of both the McAuleys (See McAuley) and McDonalds (See McDonald).

McCauley (48) See McAuley.

McCausland (2) *Scots Gaelic*. This clan acquired the island of Clarinch in Loch Lomond in 1225 which later became the gathering place of Clan Buchanan. McCauslands came to Tyrone in the 17th century.

McCay (26) *Scots Gaelic*. Meaing son of Hugh this clan came to prominence in Sutherland in the 13th century. The Mackays were also septs of Clan Davidson in Inverness-shire and of Clan Donald in Kintyre. The first Mackays or McCays to settle in Ireland, also known as McCoy (See McCoy), were Clan Donald galloglass (mercenary soldiers).

McChrystal (7) *Scots Gaelic*. Meaning son of Christopher this name was particularly associated with Galloway. Introduced to Ulster in the 17th century it is mainly found in Counties Armagh and Tyrone.

McClafferty (2) A variant of McLafferty. See Lafferty.

McClarence (1) *Scots Gaelic*. Meaning son of Laurence McClarence is a variant of MacLaren (See McLaren).

McClay (26) *Scots Gaelic*. Meaning son of the physician, and numerous in Easter and Wester Ross and in Argyll, the McClays were a sept of Clan Stewart of Appin. They frequently anglicised their name to Livingstone (See Livingstone) and Lee (See Lee).

McClea (2) A variant of McClay. See McClay.

McClean (10) *Scots Gaelic.* Meaning son of the servant of John this clan, which traces its descent from the 13th century Gillean of the Battle-axe, acquired extensive territories in Argyllshire, including the island of Mull. They came to Ulster in the 16th century as galloglasses (mercenary soldiers) to both the O'Donnells and the O'Neills.

McCleave (1) *Irish.* Also spelt as McClave and McCleve this name was anglicised to Hand in County Monaghan. McCleave was recorded in Wigtownshire, Scotland in the late 17th century.

McCleery (6) *Scots Gaelic.* Meaning son of the cleric there were septs of this name attached to Clans Campbell, Cameron, Macpherson and Mackintosh. *Irish.* A branch of the O'Haras of Sligo, who settled in County Antrim, were known as McCleary. The County Galway sept of O'Clery established itself in Derry and Donegal from the 13th century. They became regarded as a literary sept through their compilation of the famous "Annals of the Kingdom of Ireland by the Four Masters" in Donegal town. At a later date many Clearys anglicised their name to Clarke (See Clarke).

McClelland (27) *Scots Gaelic.* Meaning son of the devotee of Fillan this name was common in the Province of Galloway from the 14th century.

McClements (6) *Scots Gaelic.* As a branch of Clan Lamont McClements was one of the names adopted by members of that clan on their break-up by Clan Campbell in the late 16th century. This ancient clan which, at one time, held extensive lands in Argyll trace their descent from the O'Neills, Lords of Tyrone.

McClenaghan (5) *Irish* and *Scots Gaelic.* Meaning son of the devotee of Onchu this name was recorded in the 16th century in both County Tyrone and in Ayrshire. McClenaghan became a common name in the Province of Galloway. The name is now mainly associated with Counties Derry and Antrim.

McClintock (20) *Scots Gaelic.* Meaning son of the devotee of Fintan this name was recorded in Dunbartonshire and Argyllshire from the early 16th century. McClintock is most numerous in Counties Derry and Antrim. In some cases the name was anglicised to Lindsay. See Lindsay.

McCloskey (60) *Irish.* This County Derry sept is very much associated with the Dungiven area. They were a branch of the O'Kanes, tracing their descent from the 12th century Bloskey O'Cahan (See O'Kane).

McCloy (1) *Scottish.* In the 14th century a branch of the Fullertons (See Fullerton) settled on Arran and established the sept of McLewis which later became known as McCloy.

McClure (7) *Scots Gaelic.* Meaning son of the servant of Odhar this name has been long recorded in the Province of Galloway. In Harris in the Hebrides the McClures were a sept of Clan McLeod. It is thought that some of the McClures of County Derry are of this origin. McClure may also be a further anglicisation of the County Armagh sept name of McGillaweer.

McClurg (1) *Scots Gaelic.* Meaning son of Lurg this name was recorded in Ayrshire in the late 13th century.

McCluskey (3) See McCloskey.

McCobb (2) *Irish* or *Scots Gaelic.* Of uncertain origin this name was not recorded anywhere in County Derry in 1831. In England Cobb derived from the christian name Jacob.

McCole (1) *Irish.* Meaning son of the follower of Comhghal McCole is a variant of the County Donegal sept name of McCool (See McCool). In the Glenties area of Donegal McCole was made Cole (See Cole). *Scots Gaelic.* McCole can be a variant of MacDougall (See Duggal).

McColgan (25) *Irish.* In the 11th and 12th centuries the McColgans were the most powerful sept in the Derry area. They were a branch of Clan Dermot (See Carlin) and they were hereditary tenants of the church lands of Donaghmore in County Donegal. From the 13th century onwards the influence of the O'Kanes was to increase at the expense of the McColgans.

McCollum (1) *Irish.* Meaning son of Columcille this name was chiefly found, in the 17th century, in Counties Antrim, Donegal and Tyrone. Of similar derivation McCallum (See McCallum) was recorded as a surname in Scotland from the early 17th century.

McCombe (4) *Scots Gaelic.* Meaning son of Thomas this name was further anglicised to Holmes (See Holmes). The McCombes of Derry are mostly of Clan Mackintosh origin.

McConalogue (1) See McConnellogue.

McConnachie (1) *Scots Gaelic.* Meaning son of Duncan septs of this name were attached to Clans Campbell, MacGregor and Robertson. The name was further anglicised to Duncan (See Duncan).

McConnell (21) *Scots Gaelic.* The McConnells were a sept of the McDonnells, the Glens of Antrim branch of Clan Donald (See McDonnell).

McConnellogue (7) *Irish.* Meaning son of young Donald this sept established itself in Inishowen, County Donegal.

McConnelogue (1) See McConnellogue.

McConomey (1) See McConomy.

McConomy (13) *Irish.* A County Derry/Tyrone sept whose name meant son of the hound of Meath. The name was sometimes further anglicised to Conway (See Conway).

McConony (1) See McConomy.

McConway (4) A variant of McConomy (See McConomy). At the turn of this century Conway was still being used interchangeably with McConomy in Counties Derry and Tyrone.

McCooke (1) *Scots Gaelic.* A Clan Donald sept from Kintyre and Arran. The name was further shortened to Cooke (See Cooke).

McCool (24) *Irish.* Meaning son of the servant of Comgall this sept was based in Raphoe, County Donegal.

McCorkell (24) *Scots Gaelic.* Tracing their name from an Old Norse personal name, meaning Thor's kettle or cauldron, which became Thirkill in England, the McCorkells were a sept of Clan Gunn. In Ireland the name is mainly confined to Counties Derry and Donegal.

McCorkill (1) See McCorkell.

McCormack (4) See McCormick.

McCormick (24) *Scots Gaelic.* Meaning son of Cormac the McCormicks were a prominent sept of Clan MacLean on the island of Mull. *Irish.* A number of septs, including a branch of the

Maguries, adopted this name.

McCorriston (2) *Irish* or *Scots Gaelic*. Of uncertain origin this name was recorded in County Derry in 1831 in the parishes of Faughanvale and Magilligan. In 1796, however, there was no reference to the name anywhere in County Derry.

McCourt (22) *Irish*. This name is most numerous in Counties Antrim, Armagh and Monaghan. This is to be expected as a sept of this name originated in South Armagh. In County Monaghan the name was further anglicised to Courtney.

McCoy (1) *Scots Gaelic*. Meaning son of Hugh the McCoys were a sept of Clan Donald who came over to Ulster from Kintyre to fight for the McDonnells of the Glens of Antrim. The name has become indistinguishable from McKay (see McCay).

McCracken (5) *Scots Gaelic*. This variant of the Argyllshire clan name of McNaughten was recorded in Galloway from the early 16th century. Meaning son of Nechtan this clan claims descent from the 10th century Pictish King, Nachtan Mor.

McCrae (1) *Scots Gaelic*. Known as "MacKenzies Shirt of Mail" this clan, from the 14th century, acted as hereditary bodyguards to Clan MacKenzie in Ross. The name also sprang up independently in other parts of Scotland, including Ayrshire.

McCreadie (1) See McCready.

McCready (20) *Irish*. A County Donegal sept who were hereditary tenants of the church lands of Tullaghobegley parish.

McCrossan (8) See Crossan.

McCrudden (9) *Irish*. Meaning son of Rodan this County Donegal sept also anglicised their name to Rodden.

McCrystal (4) See McChrystal.

McCullagh (5) *Irish*. Meaning son of the hound of Ulster this name originated east of the River Bann in the ancient Kingdom of Dal Riata (See McNally). Today the name is most numerous in Counties Antrim, Down and Tyrone. *Scots Gaelic*. McCullagh was recorded in Wigtown in the late 13th century. In Oban in Argyllshire the McCullaghs were a sept of Clan Dougall.

McCullogh (1) See McCullagh.

McCully (4) A variant of McCullagh. See McCullagh.

McCune (1) *Scots Gaelic.* Meaning son of Ewen this Galloway name was first recorded there in the 14th century.

McCurdy (5) *Scots Gaelic.* As a variant of McMurtry, meaning son of Murtagh, this sept of Clan Stuart of Bute inhabited the Isles of Arran and Bute. Many settled along the North Antrim coast, including Rathlin Island, in the mid-16th century. In Scotland McCurdy was frequently anglicised to Currie (See Curry).

McCusker (3) *Irish.* This name can be a further anglicisation of Cosgrove (See Cosgrove). In addition the County Armagh sept of McIlcosker and the County Fermanagh sept of McOscar, a branch of the Maguires, became McCusker.

McDade (2) See McDaid.

McDaid (105) *Irish.* This County Donegal sept was a branch of the Dohertys. Meaning son of David they take their name from the O'Doherty chief of that name who died in 1208. In a few cases McDaid may be a variant of the Scottish clan name Davidson (See Davidson).

McDermott (59) *Irish.* This County Roscommon sept was a branch of the O'Connors, Kings of Connaught before the Norman invasions of the 12th century. A few may be of Scottish origin as in Perthshire there was a Clan Campbell sept of this name.

McDevitt (16) A variant of McDaid. See McDaid.

McDonagh (6) *Irish.* Stemming from the personal name Donagh, meaning brown warrior, septs of the name originated in County Sligo as a branch of the O'Flahertys and in County Cork as a branch of the McCarthys.

McDonald (11) *Scots Gaelic.* In historical times Clan Donald trace their lineage to 12th century Somerled, Lord of Argyll who expelled the Norsemen from the Western Isles. Folk lore traces their descent back to the semi-legendary Irish King, Conn of the Hundred Battles. They take their name from Donald, a grandson of Somerled. As Lord of the Isles with territory stretching from the Outer Hebrides to Kintyre the McDonalds became the most powerful clan in Scotland. The Lordship was broken up by the Scottish Crown in 1493. Throughout the 17th century they vied with the Campbells for the position of "Headship of the Gael". In Ireland McDonalds were recorded as galloglasses (mercenary soldier) in Tyrone from the end of the 13th century.

McDonnell (5) *Scots Gaelic.* By the mid-16th century this branch of Clan Donald (See McDonald) held extensive territory in the Glens of Antrim at the expense of the McQuillans. *Irish.* A sept with origins in County Fermanagh who were forced by the Maguires to move to Monaghan where they became sub-chiefs to the McMahons.

McDonough (2) See McDonagh.

McDowell (22) *Scots Gaelic.* Meaning son of the black foreigner the McDowells descend from Duggal, the son of Somerled who was the founder of Clan Donald (See McDonald and Duggal).

McDuff (1) *Scots Gaelic.* This clan ruled the old Earldom of Fife. In addition to having the privilege of crowning the Kings of Scotland they also led the Scottish army into battle.

Mace (1) *English.* This name derived from the biblical name Matthew during the Middle Ages.

McEleavy (1) A County Down variant of Dunlevy (See Dunleavy).

McElenay (1) A variant of McElhinney (See McElhinney) which, in 1831, was recorded largely in Glendermot parish, County Derry.

McEleneney (1) A variant of McElhinney. See McElhinney.

McEleney (11) A variant of McElhinney. see McElhinney.

McElhinney (22) *Irish.* Meaning son of the devotee of Canice this County Derry sept can trace their lineage to Eoghan, son of the 5th century Niall of the Nine Hostages.

McElholm (2) *Irish.* Meaning son of the follower of Columcille this name became established in the area between Enniskillen in County Fermanagh and Castlederg in County Tyrone.

McElome (1) A variant of McElholm. See McElholm.

McElroy (1) *Irish.* Meaning son of the red-haired youth this sept, of some importance in the 15th century, originated in County Fermanagh on the east side of Lough Erne. *Scots Gaelic.* Septs of this name belonged to Clans Grant and MacGillivray. McElroy was recorded in Dumfriesshire in 1376.

McElvenney (1) A variant of McIlwaine. See McIlwaine.

McElwee (2) *Irish.* Meaning son of the yellow-haired youth this sept originated in County Donegal. The name was also anglicised to McGilloway and McKelvey.

McErlane (1) See McErlean.

McErlean (2) *Irish.* Meaning son of the learned man this County Sligo sept settled at an early date in County Derry in Tamlaght O'Crilly parish. As early as the 12th century some ot this sept migrated to Scotland.

McEvoy (4) *Irish.* Meaning son of the woodman and originating in County Westmeath the McEvoys settled at an early date in County Leix where they became known as one of the Seven Septs of Leix. In Ulster McEvoy can, in some cases, be a corruption of either McElwee (See McElwee) or McVeigh (See McVeigh).

McEwan (1) *Scots Gaelic.* This clan held lands along Loch Fyne in Argyll until the Campbells gained possession of it in 1513. The McEwans then became a broken clan and scattered to other districts. McEwan can also be a variant of McKeown (See McKeown).

McFadden (33) *Irish.* Meaning son of Patrick this sept originated in West Donegal. *Scots Gaelic.* This sept of Clan MacLean (See McClean) was first recorded in Kintyre in 1304. On the Isle of Mull they were known as the race of the goldsmiths.

McFarland (15) *Irish.* Meaning son of Bartholomew this sept of noted poets, based in South Armagh, was first recorded in the 15th century. *Scots Gaelic.* Tracing their descent from the ancient Earls of Lennox Clan McFarlane inhabited lands on the western shores of Loch Lomond in Dunbartonshire. Owing to their war-like tendencies the clan was proscribed and dispossessed of its lands in the late 16th century.

McFaul (8) *Scots Gaelic.* Meaning son of Paul septs of this name belonged to Clans Cameron, Mackay and Mackintosh. *Irish.* The County Donegal sept name of Mulfoyle was often anglicised to McFall.

McFeeley (2) *Irish.* This name originated in the Derry/Donegal area. In 1831 it was very well established in County Derry to the west of the River Roe. McFeeley is quite distinct from the County Cork sept name of O'Feely or Fehilly.

McFeely (16) See McFeeley.

McFeeters (4) *Irish.* Meaning son of Peter this sept originated in Counties Derry and Tyrone. McFeeters was often anglicised to Peterson.

McFetridge (1) *Scots Gaelic.* Meaning son of Peter this Galloway name was often anglicised to Paterson (See Paterson).

McFrederick (1) *Scots Gaelic.* Recorded in Galloway McFrederick was a variant of McFetridge (See McFetridge).

McGahan (1) *Irish.* This well known County Louth name is also found in County Antrim and North Derry where some of the name may originally have been O'Cahon (See O'Kane).

McGahey (4) *Irish.* Derived from an old personal name which was anglicised to Aghy this spelling of the name is associated with counties Antrim and Monaghan (See McCaughey).

McGandy (2) *Scots Gaelic.* A variant of MacAndie which was both a Highland Border name and a small sept on the Island of Bernera in the Sound of Harris.

McGarrigle (11) *Irish.* Mainly associated with County Donegal McGarrigle is a variant of the County Cavan/Leitrim name McGirl. This name was also anglicised to Cargill (See Cargill).

McGarvey (6) *Irish.* This sept originated in County Donegal. Today the name is virtually confined to Counties Derry and Donegal. Garveys in Ulster are usually derived from two distinct septs of O'Garvey which originated in Counties Armagh and Down.

McGaughey (2) *Irish.* Derived from an old personal name which was anglicised to Aghy this spelling of the name is associated with Counties Armagh and Antrim (See McCaughey).

McGavigan (4) A recorded variant of both McGuigan (See McGuigan) and of the County Westmeath sept name of Geoghegan.

McGaw (1) *Irish.* Meaning son of Adam this sept originated in County Cavan. *Scots Gaelic.* Recorded as a surname in Scotland in the late 15th century the McGaws were a branch of Clan MacFarlane.

McGeady (19) *Irish.* Originating in Northwest Donegal this surname was recorded in Derry in 1831.

McGee (5) See Magee.

McGeehan (11) *Irish.* Originating in County Donegal McGeehan is now indistinguishable from McGahan in that county (See McGahan).

McGerigal (1) See McGarrigle.

McGettigan (3) *Irish.* Originating in County Tyrone this sept were chiefs of Clan Dermot in 1132 (See Carlin). The McGettigans moved westwards over time into Donegal where the name is chiefly found today.

McGhee (3) See Magee.

McGighey (1) It may be a variant of McGaughey (See McGaughey).

McGill (12) *Scots Gaelic.* Meaning son of the stranger or Lowlander this surname was common in Galloway. McGills from Jura settled in Antrim from the 14th century. *Irish.* Many Irish septs adopted the prefix Mac Gille which meant son of the follower (e.g. MacGilpatrick meant son of the follower of Patrick). At a later date, in many cases, the prefix (i.e. McGill) became the surname itself.

McGillan (2) See Gillen.

McGilligan (2) *Irish.* A County Derry sept who in the early 17th century were one of the chief septs under the O'Kanes. Their territory is known to us today as Magilligan. The name has become confused with McGillen (See Gillen).

McGilloway (39) A variant of McElwee. See McElwee.

McGinley (38) *Irish.* This County Donegal sept played an important part in church affairs in the Diocese of Raphoe. The name is often confused with McKinley (See McKinley).

McGinn (3) *Irish.* This sept originated in North Armagh but the name is now most numerous in Counties Tyrone and Down. In County Down the name tends to be spelt Maginn.

McGinnes (1) See McGuinness.

McGinnis (2) See McGuinness.

McGinty (9) *Irish.* Originating in County Donegal this sept name is now chiefly found in the south eastern part of that county bordering on Tyrone and Fermanagh. McGinty is also common in County Mayo owing to the migration of many Donegal families to Connaught during the 17th century.

McGirr (1) *Irish.* This County Tyrone sept which originated in the Clogher valley trace their descent from the 14th century "Malachy the son of the short fellow McCawell". The McCawells, a leading sept in Tyrone in the 12th century, can trace their descent from

Eoghan, son of the 5th century Niall of the Nine Hostages.

McGlinchey (16) *Irish.* Originating in County Donegal, and also anglicising their name to McClinchy, this sept name is chiefly found today in Counties Derry, Donegal and Tyrone.

McGlinchy (2) See McGlinchey.

McGlynn (2) *Irish.* Originating in the Westmeath/Roscommon area this sept spread to the west of the Shannon and north into Donegal.

McGoldrick (3) *Irish.* This sept, with origins in County Leitrim, was a branch of the O'Rourkes, Lords of Breffny. The name is now numerous in County Fermanagh. In County Donegal the name is spelt McGolrick and McGoulrigg. In County Mayo especially McGoldrick was anglicised to Golden (See Golden).

McGonagle (14) *Irish.* This County Donegal sept were hereditary tenants of the church lands at Killybegs. This sept provided two Bishops to the Diocese of Raphoe.

McGonigle (6) See McGonagle.

McGonnagle (1) See McGonagle.

McGonnigle (1) See McGonagle.

McGookin (1) A variant of McGuigan. See McGuigan.

McGovern (1) *Irish.* A County Cavan sept who trace their descent from the O'Rourkes, rulers of the ancient Kingdom of Breffny.

McGowan (53) *Irish.* Meaning son of the smith the most powerful sept of this name originated in County Cavan. Other septs of the name were also based at Inishmacsaint, County Donegal and at Clogher, County Tyrone. *Scots Gaelic.* As the maker of arms the smith was an important hereditary position in each clan. As a consequence the surname Smith was associated with most clans. This surname, more than any other, has suffered at the hands of anglicisation. Many Smiths in Ulster today were originally McGowan (See Smith).

McGranaghan (1) *Irish.* This sept originated in Mevagh in Northwest Donegal.

McGrath (6) *Irish.* This sept, with origins in County Donegal, was forced to settle at Ardstraw in County Tyrone by the O'Donnells. McGraths also originated in County Clare where they were hereditary poets to the O'Briens.

McGreanery (1) *Irish* or *Scots Gaelic*. Of uncertain origin it may disguise a number of Irish sept names such as McGranaghan (See McGranaghan) or Green (See Green).

McGregor (3) *Scots Gaelic*. The MacGregors can trace their descent from Kenneth MacAlpine, the 9th century King of Scotland. This clan came to control large territories in Perthshire and Argyllshire but in doing so they came into conflict with the powerful Clan Campbell. In the early 17th century Clan MacGregor was outlawed by the Crown and their name was proscribed. They, therefore, adopted new names (see Greer and Gregg).

McGrellis (6) *Irish*. This is a recorded variant of McNelis (See McNelis).

McGrenera (1) See McGreanery.

MacGrianna (1) *Irish*. This Gaelic surname has largely been anglicised to Green (See Green). In 1602 the MacGriannas were recorded as followers of Rory O'Donnell.

McGriskin (1) *Irish*. This sept originated in County Leitrim.

McGristan (1) A variant of McGriskin . See McGriskin.

McGroarty (3) *Irish*. Originating in County Donegal this sept were keepers of the psalter of Columcille. The townland of Ballymagroarty in the suburbs of Derry city bears their name.

McGrory (17) *Irish*. Meaning son of Rory there were two septs of the name in Ulster. A County Derry sept were hereditary tenants of the churchlands of Ballynascreen while in Fermanagh the McGrorys were a branch of the Maguires. *Scots Gaelic*. They were an important Clan Donald sept, some of whom came to Ulster as galloglasses (mercenary soldiers) in the early 14th century.

McGrotty (7) *Irish*. Confined largely to Counties Derry and Tyrone this sept name was especially prominent in the Coleraine area in 1831.

McGuigan (6) *Irish*. Tracing their descent from Eoghan, son of the 5th century Niall of the Nine Hostages this County Tyrone sept were hereditary tenants of the church lands of Ballinderry. Some of the name migrated to Scotland and settled in Kintyre at an early date.

McGuiness (5) See McGuinness.

McGuinness (27) *Irish*. Meaning son of Angus this powerful sept, based at Rathfriland, controlled most of County Down as Lords of Iveagh from the 12th century to the 17th century plantation. In some cases McGuinness is a variant of the Scottish clan name MacInnes. Also meaning son of Angus this clan traces its origins to the Irish Celts from Eastern Ulster who settled in Argyll from the 1st century A.D.

McGuire (2) See Maguire.

McGurk (3) *Irish.* Tracing their descent from the 5th century Niall of the Nine Hostages this County Tyrone sept were hereditary tenants of the church lands of Termonmaguirk.

McHale (1) *Irish.* Originating in County Mayo this sept were hereditary tenants of the church lands of Killala. A Welsh family of Howell, who settled in Mayo in the 13th century, adopted the name McHale.

McHugh (8) *Irish.* Meaning son of Hugh two distinct septs of the name originated in County Galway, one of whom were a branch of the O'Flahertys. The McHughs of Donegal may be descended from the Maguires of Fermanagh.

McIlroy (1) See McElroy.

McIlveen (1) *Irish.* A sept of this name originated in South Down. *Scots Gaelic.* A variant of McIlwaine (See McIlwaine).

McIlwaine (6) *Scots Gaelic.* Originating as a sept of Clan MacBain (See McBain) McIlwaine was a common name in Ayrshire and Galloway. *Irish.* Meaning son of the white youth a sept of this name originated in County Sligo.

McIlwee (1) See McElwee.

McIntosh (6) *Scots Gaelic.* Meaning son of the chief this clan, which claims descent from Clan MacDuff (See McDuff), were captains of the Clan Chattan confederation of clans in the 14th century from their homeland in Nairn.

McIntyre (37) *Scots Gaelic.* Meaning son of the carpenter this clan settled at Lorn in Argyllshire from the Hebrides around 1400. A branch of the family were hereditary pipers to the chiefs of Clan Menzie. The name has become much confused with McAteer (See McAteer). In the Glens of Antrim McIntyre was frequently anglicised to Wright.

McIver (1) See McIvor.

McIvor (21) *Irish.* This County Derry sept derived its name from the Norse personal name Ivar. *Scots Gaelic.* In addition to Clan McIver which acquired lands in Argyll in the 13th century there were septs of the name belonging to Clans Campbell, Robertson and MacKenzie.

McKane (6) *Scots Gaelic.* Chiefly found in County Derry McKane is a variant of McKean which was formerly known as McIan. There were McIan septs attached to both Clan Gunn and Clan Donald of Glencoe. McKean was further anglicised to Johnston (See Johnston).

McKay (7) See McCay.

McKean (3) See McKane.

McKeane (1) See McKane.

McKeating (1) *Irish.* This surname seems to have originated in the Downpatrick area, County Down. It is not to be confused with Keating which was the name borne by a Norman family who settled in County Wexford in the 12th century.

McKee (8) *Scots Gaelic.* Another anglicisation of the original name of Clan Mackay, which meant son of Hugh (See McCay). Some may also be a variant of Irish McHugh (See McHugh).

McKeefrey (1) *Irish.* This variant of the Ulster sept name of McKeaghery, which traces its descent from Niall of the Nine Hostages, was associated with County Tyrone.

McKeegan (10) *Irish.* The sept names of Keegan or McKeegan originated in two widely separated areas, namely in Counties Wicklow and Dublin and in Counties Leitrim and Roscommon. It is claimed that the McKeegans of North Uist in the Western Isles of Scotland arrived there from Ireland around 1600.

McKeever (25) A variant of McIvor (See McIvor). Some of the name, however, may descend from a branch of the McMahons of County Monaghan.

McKendrick (2) *Scots Gaelic.* Meaning son of Henry this name was further anglicised to Henderson (See Henderson). The McKendricks were a sept of Clan MacNaughton.

McKendry (1) A variant of McKendrick (See McKendrick).

McKenna (13) *Irish.* This County Meath sept settled at an early date in County Monaghan where they became Lords of Truagh. A few may be of Scottish origin as the name was recorded in Galloway in the 17th century.

Mackenzie (4) *Scots Gaelic*. This clan acquired the lands of Kintail in Ross and Cromarty in the 14th century. During the 16th century they fought on the side of three Scottish monarchs: James IV, James V and Queen Mary.

McKenzie (1) See Mackenzie.

McKeone (1) See McKeown.

McKeown (4) *Irish*. Meaning son of John various septs adopted this name. The major sept of the name was based in Sligo, but other known septs of McKeown originated in Counties Armagh and Fermanagh.

McKerr (1) A variant of McGirr. See McGirr.

Mackey (10) See McCay.

McKie (2) See McKee.

McKimm (1) *Scots Gaelic*. Meaning son of Simon the McKimms were a branch of Clan Frazer. In Ulster the name is chiefly found in County Derry.

McKimmon (1) *Irish* and *Scots Gaelic*. A gaelicised form of Fitzsimon. The Fitzsimons came to Ireland from England in the 14th century.

McKinley (5) *Scots Gaelic*. Meaning son of the fair hero septs of this name belonged to Clans Buchanan, Farquharson, MacFarlane and Stewart of Appin. This name was also anglicised to Finlay (See Finlay).

McKinney (36) *Irish*. There was a County Tyrone sept of this name. In some cases McKinney was a variant of McKenna (See McKenna). *Scots Gaelic*. Another name for Clan MacKinnon which claimed descent from Kenneth MacAlpine the 9th century King of Scotland. The clan held lands in Mull and Skye. In Ulster some Scottish MacKenzies adopted the name McKinney.

McKitterick (1) *Irish*. Derived from an Old Norse personal name this sept originated in Counties Armagh and Monaghan. In these counties McKitterick was anglicised to Hanson (See Hansen). *Scots Gaelic*. Recorded as a surname from the late 14th century

McKitterick was a common Galloway name.

McKittrick (4) See McKitterick.

McKnight (12) *Scots Gaelic.* A sept of Clan MacNaughten. Members of this clan settled in the Glens of Antrim alongside the MacDonnells in the early 17th century.

McLain (1) See McClean.

McLaren (4) *Scots Gaelic.* Claiming descent from Lorn who landed in Argyll from Ireland in 503 A.D. this clan acquired the lands of Balquhidder in Perthshire in the 12th century.

McLaughlan (1) See McLaughlin.

McLaughlin (246) *Irish.* The second most popular name in Derry. Derived from the Norse personal name Lachlann this County Donegal sept can trace its lineage to Eoghan, son of the 5th century Niall of the Nine Hostages. In the 12th century the McLaughlins, from their Inishowen homeland, were the High Kings of Ireland and patrons of the monastic settlement in Derrry. From the mid-13th century the O'Neills of Tyrone ousted the McLaughlins as the leading power in Ulster. Some may be of Scottish descent from Clan MacLachlan of Argyll.

McLean (7) See McClean.

McLeer (1) *Irish.* A variant of the County Tyrone sept name of McAleer.

MacLeod (1) *Scots Gaelic.* Tracing their descent from Leod, son of Olave the Black, King of the Isles in the 13th century this clan ruled Lewis and much of the Isle of Skye.

McLeod (1) See MacLeod.

McLery (1) A variant of McCleery. See McCleery.

McLoone (8) *Irish.* This variant of McGlone was formerly unique to Glenties in County Donegal. Meaning son of the servant of John this name, also recorded as McGloin and McGloon, originated in Counties Donegal and Tyrone. **McLorn** (1) *Irish.* A variant of the County Down sept name of McLarnon. *Scots Gaelic.* A variant of MacLaren, a clan which held lands in Perthshire and the Isle of Tiree (See McLaren).

McLoughlin (8) See McLaughlin.

McLucas (2) *Scots Gaelic.* First recorded as a surname in Inverness in the early 15th century McLucas was frequently anglicised to Douglas in Argyllshire (See Douglas) and to MacDougall in the Isles (See Duggal).

McMackin (1) *Irish.* This sept's ancient homeland was County Monaghan. McMackin is quite distinct from the County Mayo sept name of O'Mackin.

MacMahon (1) See McMahon.

McMahon (9) *Irish.* There were two distinct septs of the name. In Ulster the McMahons ruled County Monaghan from the decline of the O'Carrolls in the early 13th century. In West Clare the McMahons were a branch of the O'Briens.

McManus (7) *Irish.* Meaning son of Manus, from the Norse name Magnus, there were two septs of the name. The County Roscommon sept were kin of the O'Connors of Connaught while in County Fermanagh the McManuses were a branch of the Maguires. *Scots Gaelic.* A sept of Clan Colquohon (See Colhoun).

McMaster (1) *Scots Gaelic.* Meaning son of the master i.e. cleric, septs of the name were attached to Clans Buchanan and MacInnes. The name was chiefely found in Dumfriesshire and Wigtownshire. *Irish.* A County Cavan sept, who, in most cases, had anglicised their name to Masterson by the mid-17th century.

McMenamin (28) *Irish.* This County Donegal sept were followers of the O'Donnells. Concentrated around Letterkenny and Ballybofey the name is largely confined to Donegal and West Tyrone.

McMichael (3) *Scots Gaelic.* Meaning son of the servant of Michael there were septs of the name belonging to Clan Stewart of Appin and Clan Stewart of Galloway. The name was further anglicised to Carmichael (See Carmichael) and Mitchell (See Mitchell).

McMillan (2) *Scots Gaelic.* Meaning son of the bald one, which referred to a religious tonsure, this clan acquired the lands of Knapdale in Argyllshire in the 14th century. In Ulster this name frequently became McMullan (See McMullan).

McMillen (1) See McMillan.

McMonagle (35) *Irish.* This sept name is very much associated with County Donegal where it is now one of the most common surnames. In a few instances the prefix Mac was dropped.

McMongle (1) See McMonagle.

McMoniele (1) See McMonagle.

McMonigle (2) See McMonagle.

McMorris (10) *Irish.* It can be a gaelicised form of Fitzmaurice, the Norman family who became Lords of Lixnaw in County Kerry. In County Mayo another Norman family called Prendergast adopted McMorris as their surname.

McMorrow (1) *Irish.* This County Leitrim sept were a branch of the O'Rourkes.

McMullan (13) *Scots Gaelic.* This variant of McMillan (See McMillan) was adopted by Scottish planters in Ulster as a means to distinguish themselves from native O'Mullan (See Mullan). Understandably there can be confusion between McMullan, O'Mullan and Mullan.

McNabb (4) *Scots Gaelic.* Meaning son of the abbot this clan, which traces their descent from Kenneth MacAlpine, the 9th century King of Scotland, held lands in Perthshire. Alongside the MacDougalls they fought against Robert the Bruce in the early 14th century.

McNally (4) *Irish.* Meaning son of the hound of Ulster this name originated east of the River Bann in the ancient Kingdom of Dal Riata. Under increasing pressure from the expanding dynasties, claiming descent from Niall of the Nine Hostages, the peoples of East Ulster began to settle in Scotland. By the 6th century A.D. they had founded a colony in Argyll. McNally has the same meaning as McCullgah (See McCullagh).

McNamara (3) *Irish.* Meaning son of the hound of the sea this County Clare sept were marshalls to the O'Briens.

McNamee (6) *Irish.* Meaning son the the hound of Meath this County Tryone sept were poets to the O'Neills. A branch of the family were hereditary tenants of the church lands of Cumber Claudy in County Derry.

McNaney (1) *Irish.* A variant of McEneany, a sept name which originated in both Counties Monaghan and Roscommon. (See McAnaney).

NcNatt (1) A variant of McNaught. See McNaught.

McNaught (5) *Scots Gaelic.* This variant of McKnight (See McKnight) was recorded in Dumfriesshire in 1296.

McNaul (4) A variant of McNally. See McNally.

McNee (1) *Scots Gaelic.* Meaning son of the king the McNees were a sept of Clan MacGregor in Perthshire. The name was further anglicised to King (See King).

McNeill (10) *Scots Gaelic.* Claiming descent from one Niall, twenty-first in descent from the 5th century High King of Ireland, Niall of the Nine Hostages, this clan settled in Barra in the Outer Hebrides in 1049. In the 14th century McNeills came to Ulster as galloglasses (mercenary soldiers) and settled in Counties Derry and Antrim. They were Lords of Clandeboy for a while before submitting to the O'Neills in the late 15th century.

McNelis (1) *Irish.* Originating as a sept in County Donegal their name is recorded as both McNelis and Nelis. McNelis tends to be peculiar to Donegal whereas Nelis is found in adjoining counties.

McNerlin (1) A variant of McErlean. See McErlean.

McNicholl (2) *Irish.* A County Tyrone sept whose name was also recorded as McNickle. *Scots Gaelic.* Clan MacNicol settled in Skye from the 14th century where they were sub-lords of Clan MacLeod. Owing to the further anglicisation of these names to Nicholls and Nicholson, which are forms that originated in England from the Latin name Nicholas, the exact origins of this name and its many variants can cause confusion.

McNickle (1) See McNicholl.

McNulty (13) *Irish.* Meaning son of the Ulsterman this sept originated in South Donegal. One of the names assumed by the Dunleavys (See Dunleavy) when they settled in Donegal was McNulty.

McNutt (8) *Scots Gaelic.* This corruption of McNaught (See McNaught) was adopted in Ulster.

Maconachie (1) See McConnachie.

McOwan (1) A variant of McKeown. See McKeown.

McParland (2) A variant of McFarland. See McFarland.

McPartland (1) A variant of McFarland. See McFarland.

McPartlin (1) A variant of McFarland . See McFarland.

McPeake (1) *Irish.* Originating in South Derry this sept's name is perpetuated in the townland name Ballymacpeake, near the town of

Maghera, County Derry.

McPherson (5) *Scots Gaelic*. Meaning son of the parson Clan MacPherson, from their base at Cluny in Inverness-shire, fought with Clan Mackintosh for leadership of the Clan Chattan confederation of clans.

McPhilemy (1) *Irish*. Meaning son of Phelim this sept originated in County Tyrone.

McPhillips (2) *Scots Gaelic*. Meaning son of Philip, and found mainly in Counties Cavan and Monaghan, the McPhillips were a branch of Clan MacDonnell.

McQuade (1) See McQuaid.

McQuaid (4) *Irish*. This sept originated in County Monaghan and by the 17th century the name was established in County Armagh. McQuaid and its variants were sometimes corrupted to McWade and Wade.

McQuaide (2) See McQuaid.

McQuilkin (2) *Scots Gaelic*. Meaning son of Wilkin this sept, which was based in Kintyre and Islay, anglicised their name to Wilkinson (See Wilkinson).

McReynolds (2) See Reynolds.

McRory (1) See McGrory.

McShane (15) *Irish*. Meaning son of John this sept, based in Northeast Tyrone, was a branch of the O'Neills. The name was frequently anglicised to Johnson (See Johnston).

McSheffrey (3) *Irish*. This is the gaelic form of Jeffries and Jefferson (See Jeffrey) and it is mainly found in Counties Derry and Donegal.

McSherry (3) *Irish*. Meaning son of Geoffrey this sept originated in County Armagh. In written documents of the 12th century to the 17th century the name was recorded as both McSherry and O'Sherry. In Scotland McSherry was recorded on both Skye and Mull in the 17th century.

McSorley (2) *Scots Gaelic*. Meaning son of Somerled, which was a Norse name, there were septs of this name attached to Clans Cameron, Lamont and Donald. From the 13th century McSorleys came to Ulster as galloglasses (mercenary soldiers) to the McDonnells of Antrim.

McSparran (1) *Scots Gaelic.* In Scotland this branch of Clan Donald was known as McSporran. They were hereditary purse-bearers to the Lords of the Isles. The name is now fairly numerous in Counties Derry and Antrim.

McSparron (1) See McSparran.

McSwiggan (1) *Scots Gaelic.* Now mainly found in Tyrone this Galloway name was ultimately of Irish origin.

McSwine (1) A variant of Sweeney. See Sweeney.

McTaggart (2) *Irish* and *Scots Gaelic.* Meaning son of the priest a sept of this name established itself in Fermanagh while in Scotland McTaggart frequently appears in records from the late 15th century. The name was often abbreviated to Taggart (See Taggart).

McTernan (2) *Irish.* Originating in County Cavan and West Leitrim this sept was of some importance throughout the period 1250 to 1550. In County Roscommon a sept known as McTiernan established itself.

McVeigh (5) *Scots Gaelic.* This name, also known as MacBeth in Scotland, arose in Moray where the McVeighs were allies to the MacBains. In Skye and in Islay and Mull, as a Clan Donald sept, the McVeighs were hereditary physicians to the MacDonalds, Lords of the Isles.

McWhirter (1) *Scots Gaelic.* Originally meaning son of the harper McWhirter was frequently anglicised to Harper (See Harper).

McWilliams (6) *Scots Gaelic.* Septs of this name belonged to Clans Gunn and MacFarlane. The name has become confused with McQuillan, the Norman family who ruled North Antrim from their stronghold at Dunluce castle from the late 12th century to the mid-16th century. McWilliams was also anglicised to Williamson (See Williamson).

M

Madden (5) *Irish.* This powerful sept retained the lordship of their territory in East Galway even under the Norman de Burgo (i.e. Burke) supremacy. In County Kildare an English family of the name settled there.

Madeley (1) *English.* Derived from place names in Shropshire and

Staffordshire meaning Mada's clearing.

Magee (25) *Scots Gaelic*. Meaning son of Hugh this name was first recorded in Dumfries in the 13th century. They were connected to the Clan Donald sept of Mackey (See McCay). *Irish*. Septs of this name, meaning son of Hugh, were based in: Islandmagee, County Antrim; Kilmacrenan, County Donegal; and in Fermanagh where they were a branch of the Maguires.

Magilligan (1) See McGilligan.

Maginnis (1) See McGuinness.

Magnier (1) It may be a variant of Magner. The County Cork name of Magnel, of which there were many references in the 13th century, had become Magner by the 16th century.

Magowan (5) See McGowan.

Maguinness (1) See McGuinness.

Maguire (11) *Irish*. This County Fermanagh sept established itself at Lisnaskea around 1200. By 1300 the Maguires were rulers of all Fermanagh. In a few cases the name may derive from Scotland where MacGuire was a sept of Clan MacQuarrie on the island of Ulva.

Maher (1) *Irish*. Originating in the Roscrea area of Tipperary this sept, unlike others, was not driven from their homeland after the 12th century Anglo-Norman invasion.

Mahon (11) See Vaughan and McMahon.

Mahony (2) *Irish*. This powerful sept originated in Southwest Cork where the name is mainly found today.

Mailey (6) A variant of O'Malley. See Malley.

Mairs (1) *English* and *Scottish*. Derived from the occupational names for an officer of the court in Scotland and for a Mayor in England.

Makepeace (1) *English* and *Scottish*. Derived from a nickname for a person who could arbitrate in quarrels it was recorded as a surname in Scotland from the 14th century.

Mallat (1) See Mallet.

Mallet (17) *English*. A Norman family of this name accompanied William the Conqueror to England in 1066. A Huguenot family, called Malet or Mallet, settled in Kent, in the late 18th century, and in County Cork. There are five known origins of this name with the most interesting being that of a nickname for 'a fearsome warrior'.

Malley (1) *Irish.* Originating on the coast of Mayo this sept was renowned for its maritime prowess and, in particular, for the exploits of the 16th century Grace O'Malley.

Mallon (4) A variant of Mellon. See Mellon.

Malseed (1) Found mainly in County Donegal this name is thought to be of Dutch origin.

Maltman (1) *Scottish.* Derived from the occupational name for a brewer who used malt it was recorded as a surname in Aberdeen in the early 16th century.

Mangan (1) *Irish.* There were three distinct septs of this name with origins in Counties Mayo, Limerick and Tyrone. The latter sept were hereditary tenants of the church lands of Termonamongan in West Tyrone.

Manly (1) *English.* Derived either from villages in Devon and Cheshire meaning shared clearing or as a nickname for 'a brave man'. *Irish.* A County Cork sept anglicised their name to Manly.

Mann (3) It is usually a variant of Scottish McManus (See McManus). In a few cases it may be a variant of Mahon (See McMahon).

Manning (6) *English.* Derived either from a nickname for 'a fierce or strong man' or from a Germanic personal name recorded as Manna. It may also be a variant of Mannion (See Mannion).

Mannion (1) *Irish.* Originating in County Galway, with their base being the castle of Clogher, this sept's territory was reduced in size by the O'Kellys.

Manthorpe (1) *English.* Derived from two Lincolnshire place names meaning Manni's settlement.

Maquire (1) A variant of Maguire. See Maguire.

Marchini (4) Originating from the Province of Tuscany in Northern Italy this name came to Derry, via Dublin, after the end of World War One. They worked, in the 1920s, in Cafolla's fish and chip business in the Waterside which was known as the Luxor Cafe.

Margey (1) There are 13 references to Margey in the Irish telephone directories yet the origin of this name is uncertain. The name was frequently recorded in the 19th century baptism registers of Roman Catholic parishes in Inishowen, County Donegal. Furthermore the name was recorded in County Derry in 1831 in the parishes of Cumber Upper and Tamlaght O'Crilly.

Marley (2) *English.* Derived from a number of place names a Northumbrian family of this name settled in County Longford in 1675. *Irish.* Originating in Counties Armagh and Monaghan this sept's name is now mainly found in Counties Donegal and Mayo.

Marrs (1) *English* and *Scottish.* Derived from place names in West Yorkshire and Aberdeenshire, meaning marshy land.

Marsh (1) *English.* Derived from a local name for someone who lived by or in a marsh or fen.

Marshall (8) *English* and *Scottish.* Derived as an occupational name for a horse servant. Although recorded in Ireland from the early Middle Ages most Marshalls in Ulster stem from 17th century Scottish planters.

Martin (27) Can be of *English, Scottish* or *Irish* origin. In Ireland it may be abbreviations of the County Tyrone sept name of McMartin and of the County Fermanagh sept name of McGilmartin. In England the personal name Martin became, at an early date, a popular surname while in Scotland septs of the name were attached to Clan Cameron in Inverness-shire and to Clan Donald in Skye.

Mason (8) *English* and *Scottish.* Derived from the occupational name for a stone mason. There was a prominent family of this name in the Orkney Islands in the 16th century.

Masood Originating from the Northwest Frontier Province of Afghanistan the bearer of this name came to Enniskillen in 1973.

Masterton (1) *Scottish.* Derived from the lands of Masterton in Fifeshire it was first recorded as a surname in 1296.

Matchett (2) *English.* Derived from Matthew (See Matthews) this surname is now more common in Northern Ireland than in England.

Matt (1) *English.* An abbreviated form of Matthew (See Matthews).

Matthews (3) *English* and *Scottish.* Derived from the biblical name Mathew this name is now numerous throughout Ulster. In some instances McMahon was anglicised to Matthews (See McMahon).

Matthewson (1) Like Matthews this name simply means son of Matthew (See Matthews).

Mawhinney (1) *Scots Gaelic.* A variant of MacKenzie (See Mackenzie) which was recorded in the Province of Galloway. Mawhinney may also be a variant of Sweeney (See Sweeney).

Maxwell (5) *Scottish.* This riding clan of the Scottish Borders takes its name from the lands of Maxwell, meaning Marcus's pool, which they were granted along the River Tweed in the 12th century. For centuries they feuded with the Johnstones.

Mayes (1) *English.* Derived from the personal name Mathew (See Matthews).

Maynes (1) It is usually a variant of Scottish McManus (See McManus) although in Fermanagh the native McManuses sometimes adopted the name Mayne.

Mayse (1) *English.* Derived from the personal name Mathew (See Matthews).

Meadows (1) *English.* Derived from the local name for someone who lived by a meadow.

Meehan (14) *Irish.* Septs of this name were based in Counties Clare/Galway and in Leitrim. The latter sept, a branch of the McCarthys, settled in Leitrim in the 11th century. They later spread to Fermanagh where they became hereditary tenants of the church lands of Devenish.

Meehin (1) See Meehan.

Meeman (1) Only recorded in Derry in the Northern Ireland phone book. It may be a variant of Meenan. See Meenan.

Meenagh (1) *Irish.* This variant of the County Tyrone sept name of Minnagh was sometimes anglicised to Thornton (See Thornton).

Meenan (19) *Irish.* This sept originated in County Donegal in the district between Rathmullan and Ramelton.

Megarty (1) This is a misspelling of Hegarty by British Telecom. (See Hegarty).

Mehaffey (1) *Scots Gaelic.* Meaning son of the black one of peace this sept of Clan MacFie (See Duffy) settled in Galloway from the early 17th century.

Mehaffy (1) See Mehaffey.

Melarkey (6) *Irish.* This County Donegal sept, better known as Mullarkey, migrated to Connaught in the 17th century. The name is now chiefly found in Counties Galway, Mayo and Sligo.

Melaugh (14) *Irish.* Today this name is chiefly found in the Derry area. In 1831, as Malaugh, the name was to be found in Glendermott parish.

Melican (1) *Irish.* This sept originated in West Clare. It may also be a variant of Milligan (See Milligan).

Mellon (17) *Irish.* Tracing their descent from Eoghan, son of the 5th century Niall of the Nine Hostages this sept originated to the south of the Sperrins in North Tyrone. The name has become confused with Mullan (See Mullan).

Melly (1) *Irish.* This sept originated in North Connaught and Donegal. Melly is quite distinct from Malley (See Malley).

Melrose (2) *Scottish.* Derived from the town of Melrose in Roxburghshire in the Scottish Borders, meaning barren moor it was recorded as a surname from the mid-15th century.

Mercer (3) *English* and *Scottish.* Derived from the Old French occupational name for a merchant which originally referred to a person who dealt in textile fabrics, especially silks and other costly materials.

Mernor (1) According to family tradition this name is Dutch in origin. In the Waterside of Derry City in 1898 Edward Mernor married Elizabeth Higgins.

Merrigan (3) *Irish.* This sept originated in Counties Longford and Westmeath. The name was also anglicised to Morgan (See Morgan).

Meyler (1) *Welsh.* Derived from the Old Welsh personal name of Meilyr a sept of this name traces its origins to a Welsh family who settled in County Wexford in 1200.

Michaelides (1) This is a Greek name derived from the popular European christian name of Michael.

Middleton (4) *English* and *Scottish.* Derived from a great number of place names meaning middle settlement. In Scotland a family of this name derived it from the lands of Middleton in Kincardineshire which they were granted in 1094.

Millar (23) *English* and *Scottish.* As every manor or estate had its miller this occupational surname sprang up all over England and Scotland. Millar is usually regarded as the Scottish spelling of the name.

Millen (3) An abbreviated form of McMillen (See McMillan).

Miller (28) See Millar.

Milligan (6) A variant of Mulligan. See Mulligan.

Mills (9) *English.* Derived either from a local name for someone who lived by the mills or from the Old French personal name Miles. In Scotland Mill is a corruption of Miln. (See Milne).

Milne (1) *Scottish.* Derived from a local name for someone who lived near a corn mill. Miln is a very common surname in Aberdeenshire.

Ming (4) Family tradition states that Ming may be an abbreviated form of Scottish Menzies which is pronounced Mingies.

Mitchell (41) Can be of *English, Scottish* or *Irish* origin. Derived from the Hebrew personal name Michael, and in a few cases from a nickname meaning 'big', Mitchell became very numerous throughout England and Scotland. In Northeast Scotland the Mitchells were a sept of Clan Innes. Furthermore the Highland Scottish name of McMichael (See McMichael) was frequently anglicised to Mitchell. In Ireland, and in County Donegal especially, the County Roscommon sept name of Mulvihill was anglicised to Mitchell.

Moffett (1) *Scottish.* Derived from the Dumfriesshire place name of Moffat the Moffetts were one of the smaller riding clans of the Scottish Borders.

Moffitt (1) See Moffett.

Mohamat (1) Originating from Java in Indonesia this name came to Derry, via Liverpool, in 1961.

Mollon (1) A Variant of Mullan found in County Down. See Mullan.

Molloy (19) *Irish.* Tracing their descent from the 5th century Niall of the Nine Hostages the Molloys were an important sept in County Offaly. A branch later settled in County Roscommon. Molloy has been recorded as a variant of the County Donegal name of Logue. (See Logue).

Molner (1) This variant of Miller (See Millar) can be found in Germany.

Moloney (2) *Irish.* Originating in East Clare this sept name is also found in large numbers in the adjoining counties of Limerick and Tipperary.

Monaghan (14) *Irish.* Meaning descendant of the monk the main sept of this name originated in County Roscommon. Monaghans in the Northwest, however, will trace their descent to the North Fermanagh sept of the name.

Monagle (1) See McMonagle.

Monk (3) Can be of *English, Scottish* or *Irish* origin. In England it originated as an occupational name. In Scotland the Highland sept of McManachan, meaning son of the monk, was anglicised to Monk while in Ireland Monaghan (See Monaghan) and the East Clare sept name of Minogue were anglicised to Monk.

Montague (2) *English.* Derived from a French place name meaning pointed hill. *Irish.* In Counties Armagh and Tyrone the sept name of McTague was anglicised to Montague. It was also anglicised to McCaig, McKeag and McKeague.

Monteith (3) *Scottish.* Derived from a place name in Southwest Perthshire meaning hill pasture by the River Teith. Introduced to Ulster with the 17th century plantation Monteith is now quite common in Tyrone.

Montgomery (14) *Scottish.* Tracing their descent from Roger de Montgomery, Regent of Normandy, who accompanied William the Conqueror to England in 1066 this clan acquired lands in Renfrewshire in the 12th century.

Monti (1) This Italian name is derived from a local name for someone who lived on or near a hill.

Moody (3) *English.* Derived as a nickname for 'a courageous or impetuous person'. It was introduced to Ireland in the 13th century and from the 17th century it has been mainly found in Ulster and in Armagh in particular.

Mooney (20) *Irish.* There were several distinct septs of the name, including a branch in County Donegal who were hereditiary tenants of the church lands at Ardara.

Moore (125) Can be of *English, Scottish* or *Irish* origin. In England and Scotland the name derived either from the personal name More, meaning Moor (i.e. the Muslim people of Northwest Africa) or from a local name for someone who lived on or near moorland. Moore became widespread as a surname throughout England and Scotland. In Scotland the name was also known as More and Muir.

The Mores were a sept of Clan Leslie while the Muirs were a sept of Clan Campbell. In Ireland the O'Mores were the leading sept of the Seven Septs of Leix.

Moorehead (3) *Scottish.* A Northern Irish variant of Muirhead which was derived from a number of Southern Scottish place names meaning end of the moor.

Morahan (1) *Irish.* There were two distinct septs of this name, one originating in East Offaly and the other in County Leitrim. Morahan was further anglicised to Moran (See Moran) and Morrin (See Morrin).

Moran (41) *Irish.* In the Province of Connaught there were four distinct septs of this name. In addition the County Fermanagh sept of McMorran has become Moran. Moran is also a recorded variant of Morahan (See Morahan).

More (2) See Moore.

Morgan (3) *Welsh.* Derived from the Old Welsh name Morcant meaning sea-bright. *Scottish.* Morgan was largely confined to Aberdeenshire and Sutherland. The Mackeys (See McCay) of Sutherland were also known as Clan Morgan. *Irish.* The East Offaly sept of Morahan (See Morahan) and the County Westmeath sept of Merrigan also anglicised their names to Morgan.

Moriarty (1) *Irish.* Originating in County Kerry this sept was of the same stock as the O'Donoghues and the O'Mahonys.

Morrin (2) *Irish.* It is usually a variant of either Moran (See Moran) or Morahan (See Morahan). In some cases, however, it is a Huguenot name. Many Huguenots fled to Ulster from France in the late 17th century in the face of persecution by Louis XIV.

Morris (4) Can be of *English, Scottish* or *Irish* origin. Derived from the popular Norman name Maurice, meaning Moorish (i.e. from Moor, the Muslim people of Northwest Africa) it became a very common surname in England and Scotland. In Ireland at least two septs, one originating in County Fermanagh and the other in County Sligo, anglicised their name to Morris. In addition Morris of Norman origin became one of the "Tribes of Galway".

Morrison (58) *Irish.* A County Donegal sept who were hereditary tenants of the church lands of Clonmany adopted this English name which meant son of Maurice (See Morris). *Scots Gaelic.* Claiming descent from a Norse family shipwrecked on the Island of Lewis Clan Morrison, from their seat at Habost on the northern tip of the Isle of Lewis, became sub-lords to the MacLeods.

Morrow (11) *English.* Derived from a local name for someone who lived in a row of houses on moorland. *Irish.* Meaning son of the mariner two distinct septs of McMorrow originated in Counties Fermanagh and Leitrim.

Moss (1) Can be of *English, Scottish* or *Irish* origin. In England and Scotland it derived as a local name for someone who lived by a peat bog. In Ireland Moss can be a partial translation of the gaelic sept name of Malmona which was found in Counties Fermanagh and Donegal.

Mould (1) *English.* Derived from a medieval female name, variously spelt as Mauld, Malt or Maud, which was a variant of the Norman name Matilda.

Mouncey (1) *English* and *Scottish.* Derived from Norman place names meaning hillock it was recorded as a surname in the Scottish Borders from the late 13th century.

Mount (3) *English* and *Scottish.* Derived originally from a French local name for someone who lived on or near a hill. In Scotland there were places of this name in Fifeshire, Lanarkshire and Peeblesshire.

Mountain (2) *English.* A variant of French Montagne it derived as a local name for someone who lived on or near a hill. This surname is chiefly found in Yorkshire. In Ireland the County Waterford sept name of Manton became Mountain.

Mowbray (3) *English.* Derived from the French place name of Montbrai, meaning mud hill. Norman Robert de Mowbray became Earl of Northumberland in 1080.

Moyne (2) This is a recorded variant of English Monk (See Monk). It may also be an abbreviated form of Moynihan (See Moynihan).

Moynihan (1) *Irish.* Meaning descendant of a Munsterman this sept originated in West Cork and Kerry. Minihan, Minnagh and Moyna are other forms of the name.

Muir (3) See Moore.

Mulberry (1) *Irish.* Meaning descendant of the devotee of Barry this sept originated in County Derry. It is also a recorded variant of Mowbray (See Mowbray).

Muldoon (3) *Irish.* There were three distinct septs of this name. The most important one originated in County Fermanagh where they were chiefs of Lurg. Other septs of the name established themselves in Counties Clare and Galway.

Mulgrew (1) *Irish.* Originating in County Tyrone this sept name was also anglicised to Mulcreevy. In County Armagh Mulgrew was shortened to Grew.

Mulhern (9) *Irish.* Originating in County Roscommon, where it was better known as Mulkerrin, a branch of this sept established itself in Southwest Donegal.

Mulheron (1) See Mulhern.

Mulholland (6) *Irish.* Meaning son of the devotee of Calann septs of this name originated in South Derry and County Donegal.

Mullally (1) *Irish.* Originating in County Galway this sept was constantly feuding with the de Burgos or Burkes.

Mullan (51) *Irish.* Meaning descendant of the bald one and tracing their descent from the 5th century Niall of the Nine Hostages the sept of O'Mullan originated in the Laggan district of East Donegal. As a member of Clan Connor they accompanied the O'Kanes in their invasion and settlement of North Derry in the 12th century. Confusion is caused by the fact that the majority of Scottish Macmillans (See McMillan) adopted the surname of McMullan which, like O'Mullan, was frequently shortened to Mullan.

Mullen (5) See Mullan.

Mulligan (3) *Irish.* Meaning descendant of the bald one the County Donegal sept of Mulligan were hereditary tenants of the church lands of Tullyfern. Losing their lands during the plantation the sept migrated to Fermanagh and Monaghan. *Scots Gaelic.* Milligan and its variant Milliken are common names in Galloway where they have been recorded since the late 13th century.

Mullin (4) See Mullan.

Mulrine (3) *Irish.* This County Donegal name is also recorded as Mulrain and Mulroyne in Connaught. Mulrine is distinct from the

Limerick/Tipperary sept of Mulryan which was later shortened to Ryan. Ryan is by far the most numerous name in Tipperary today. In County Carlow a small sept, distinct from Mulryan, anglicised its name to Ryan.

Mulvey (2) *Irish.* There were two distinct septs of this name; the County Leitrim sept were a branch of the O'Farrells while in County Clare the Mulveys established themselves on the Atlantic coast.

Munro (2) *Scottish.* Derived from a local name meaning mouth of the River Roe. The River Roe rises above Dungiven and flows south to Lough Foyle. Clan Munro traces its descent from Donald O'Kane who migrated with some of his kin in the 11th century from the Roe Valley, County Derry to Cromarty, Scotland.

Murie (1) See Murray.

Murphy (36) *Irish.* Meaning descendant of sea warrior three major septs of the name originated in Counties Cork, Wexford and Roscommon. In the Northwest, however, many will be descended from the County Tyrone sept of McMurphy who trace their lineage to the 5th century Niall of the Nine Hostages. In Fermanagh a branch of the Maguires took the name Murphy.

Murray (44) *Scots Gaelic.* Taking their name from the northern province of Moray this clan acquired its territory in the 12th century from David I. *Irish.* Derived from a given name meaning mariner several septs of this name originated in Counties Cork, Down, Leitrim and Roscommon.

Murray-Cavanagh (1) A double-barrelled name. See Murray and Kavanagh.

Murtland (1) *Scottish.* This variant of Morthland was derived from a place name in Ayrshire which can no longer be identified.

Myles (2) *English.* Derived either from the Germanic personal name Milo or from the occupational name for a servant. In Ireland the County Roscommon sept name of Mullery of Mulry was changed to Myles. In Scotland Myles was found as a surname in the Western Isles.

N

Nagra (3) Originating from Jullundur in the State of Punjab in Northern India this name came to Derry in 1950.

Nairn (2) *Scottish.* Derived from the town of Nairn to the east of Inverness it was first recorded as a surname in that area from the mid-14th century.

Nash (14) *English.* Derived from a local name, found in Southern England, for someone who lived by an ash tree. An Anglo-Norman family of this name settled in County Kerry in the 13th century.

Naylor (1) *English.* Derived as an occupational name for a maker of nails the first Naylors came to Dublin early in the 17th century.

Nee (1) *Irish.* The gaelic name O'Nee, meaning descendant of the hero, was anglicised to Nee in Galway, Needham in Mayo and Neville in Counties Cork and Limerick.

Neely (18) *Irish* and *Scots Gaelic.* This variant of McNeilly, meaning son of the poet, was particularly associated with County Antrim. McNeilly was established as a surname in Galloway, Scotland by the 15th century. Furthermore the County Galway sept name of Conneely was anglicised to Neely.

Neeson (2) *Irish.* This sept, whose name was also anglicised to McNeece, was established in Counties Monaghan and Tyrone by the mid-17th century.

Neff (1) A recorded variant of English Neve whch derived as a nickname meaning 'a nephew'.

Neill (1) An abbreviated form of McNeill (See McNeill) or O'Neill (See O'Neill).

Nelis (11) See McNelis.

Nelson (5) *Scottish.* Meaning son of Niall septs of this name belonged to Clans Gunn, Mackey and Stuart.

Nesbitt (5) *English* and *Scottish.* Derived from various place names, meaning nose-shaped bend, found in Berwickshire, Durham and Northumberland.

Newburn (1) *English* and *Scottish.* Derived from place names found in Northumberland and Suffolk in England and in Fifeshire and Stirlingshire in Scotland, meaning new stream. This would have denoted a stream which had changed its course.

Newton (6) *English* and *Scottish.* Derived from a great number of place names meaning new settlement. Newton is the commonest English place name and for this reason the surname originated independently all over the country. In Scotland the earliest references to the surname in the 13th century derived from the parish of Newton in Midlothian.

Nicell (9) A variant of Nicholl. See McNicholl.

Nichol (2) See McNicholl.

Nicholas (4) See McNicholl.

Nicholl (23) See McNicholl.

Nicholls (1) See McNicholl.

Nichols (1) See McNicholl.

Nicholson (2) See McNicholl.

Niven (1) *Irish.* Originating in County Galway this sept, whish was based near Loughrea, was famed both for their poets and physicians. *Scottish.* Derived from the personal name Naomh (latinised as Nevinus) which was a popular forename in Galloway and Ayrshire.

Nixon (5) *English* and *Scottish.* Meaning son of Nick, which in turn was derived from Nicholas, the Nixons were a powerful riding clan of the Scottish Borders with territory on both the English and Scottish side of the border. With the 17th century plantation they came to Fermanagh in large numbers.

Noble (4) *English* and *Scottish.* Derived from a Norman nickname meaning 'well-known or noble' the Nobles were one of the riding clans on the English side of the Scottish Borders. They were also a sept of Clan Mackintosh. Noble was recorded in Ireland from the 13th century while the 17th century plantation established the name in Fermanagh.

Nolan (4) *Irish.* Originating in County Carlow a branch of this sept migrated to East Connaught and County Longford. In Roscommon and Mayo Holohan (See Holahan) became Nolan while the County Fermanagh sept of Hultaghan was anglicised to Nolan.

Norby (1) See Norrby.

Norrby (5) *English.* Derived from the Swedish term for north settlement. By is a common second element in place names in those parts of Northern England where the Scandinavians settled. It originally denoted a village or a homestead.

Norris (20) *English* and *Scottish.* Derived from the Old French term Noreis, meaning Northerner. In the case of Ireland it originally referred to someone who had come from Scandinavia. As a surname it has been recorded in Ireland since the 13th century (See also Nurse).

North (2) *English.* Derived from a local name for someone who lived in the northern part of a village or for someone who had migrated from the North. *Irish.* A recorded variant of Dunlevy (See Dunleavy). On leaving Ulster and settling in Westmeath a branch of the Dunleavys adopted the surname North.

Nortonen (1) In all of Ireland the only reference to Nortonen in the telephone directories is in Derry.

Nugent (4) *English.* Derived from the Norman place name of Nogent the Nugents established themselves in Meath and Westmeath in the 12th century. In some cases the County Tyrone sept of Gilshenan anglicised their name to Nugent.

Nurse (1) *English.* A recorded variant of Norris (See Norris). In this case Norris derived as an occupational name for a nurse from Old French Norrice.

Nutt (10) *Irish.* An abbreviated form of McNutt. (See McNutt). *English.* Derived from a nickname for a man resembling a nut, for example by having a brown complexion.

Nutter (2) *English.* Derived from occupational names for either a keeper of oxen or for a scribe or clerk.

O

Oakes (2) *English.* Derived from a local name for someone who lived in an oak wood. *Irish.* Darragh (See Darragh) was sometimes anglicised to Oakes.

O'Boyle (4) See Boyle.

O'Brien (9) *Irish.* Denoting descent from Brian Boru, High King of

Ireland in the early 11th century, this sept controlled a great part of the Province of Munster and vied with the O'Neills and O'Connors for the High Kingship of all Ireland.

O'Bryan (1) See O'Brien.

O'Callaghan (2) See Callaghan.

O'Carolan (2) An older spelling of Carlin (See Carlin) which is nearer the original gaelic spelling of this sept name.

O'Carroll (1) See Carroll.

O'Comain (1) *Irish.* Originating in County Mayo and in Counties Cork and Tipperary this name has been anglicised to Cummins and Commons and in some cases Hurley.

O'Connell (17) *Irish.* This County Kerry sept was driven out of its homeland by the O'Donoghues in the 11th century.

O'Connor (22) *Irish.* There were at least six distinct septs of this name, including the O'Connors of Roscommon and Sligo who were High Kings of Ireland in the 12th century. The O'Connors of Derry trace their lineage to Cian, King of Munster in the 3rd century. Their territory was overrun by the O'Kanes in the 12th century.

O'Doherty (54) See Doherty.

O'Donaghue (1) See Donohoe.

O'Donghaile (1) *Irish.* This is the gaelic form of Donnelly. (See Donnelly).

O'Donnell (91) *Irish.* Taking their name from Domhnall, who died in 901, and tracing their descent from Conall Gulban, son of the 5th century Niall of the Nine Hostages, this sept, from their base around Kilmacrenan, County Donegal, rose in importance from the 13th century to the position of overlords of Donegal. The O'Donnells, alongside the O'Neills, led the Ulster Rebellion of 1594-1603 against English encroachment.

O'Donoghue (1) See Donohoe.

O'Driscoll (1) *Irish.* This sept established itself in County Cork but it later lost part of its territory to the O'Mahonys and the O'Donovans.

O'Dwyer (1) *Irish.* This important sept in County Tipperary were noted for their resistance to English rule in the Middle Ages.

O'Farrell (1) See Farrell.

O'Flaherty (1) *Irish.* This sept, under pressure from the Norman invader, in the 13th century moved westwards from its territory on the east side of Lough Corrib and established itself on the western seaboard of County Galway. In Ulster Flaherty often became Lafferty. (See Lafferty).

Ogilby (1) *Scottish.* This clan acquired the lands of Ogilvy in Angus in 1163. In its home country this name is better known as Ogilvy. In some cases McElwee (See McElwee) was anglicised to O'Gilvie and then to Ogilvy.

Ogilvie (1) See Ogilby.

O'Grady (2) *Irish.* This sept originated in County Clare. In the late 16th century a branch of the family changed its name to Brady (See Brady). In addition the Mayo name of McGready has been corrupted to O'Grady.

O'Hagan (36) *Irish.* This County Tyrone sept, with their base at Tullahogue, can trace their lineage to Eoghan, son of the 5th century Niall of the Nine Hostages. They held the hereditary right of inaugurating the O'Neills as Kings of Ulster.

O'Hara (10) *Irish.* Originating in County Sligo a branch of this sept migrated to the Glens of Antrim in the 14th century.

O'Hare (2) *Irish.* Kin to the O'Hanlons (See Hanlon) this sept was based in central Armagh.

O'Hea (3) *Irish.* Meaning descendant of Hugh this sept originated in Southwest Cork and even to this day the name is largely confined to this county (See Hayes).

O'Kane (55) *Irish.* The sept of O'Kane or O'Cahon can trace their lineage to Eoghan, son of the 5th century Niall of the Nine Hostages. Originating in the Laggan district of County Donegal the O'Kanes, who were the leading sept of Clan Connor, settled in the Dungiven area from the 10th century. By the 12th century they had established themselves in County Derry from the Foyle to the Bann and they had gained the privilege of inaugurating the chief of the O'Neills.

O'Kelly (2) See Kelly.

O'Laifeartaigh (1) *Irish.* This is the gaelic form of Lafferty. (See Lafferty).

O'Leary (5) *Irish.* With Norman incursions of the late 12th century this sept, which originated in Southwest Cork, migrated to Muskerry in North Cork.

O'Loughlin (3) *Irish.* Quite distinct from McLaughlin this sept originated in Northwest Clare where they were Lords of Burren.

Olphert (11) *Scottish.* This variant of Oliphant is chiefly found in Counties Antrim and Derry. The Oliphants of Norman origin, who settled in Northamptonshire in the late 11th century, acquired lands in Roxburghshire in the 12th century.

O'Neill (50) *Irish.* Tracing their descent from Eoghan, son of the 5th century Niall of the Nine Hosatages, this sept has one of the oldest surnames in Ireland. It has been in continuous use since King Domhnall in the 10th century adopted the name of his grandfather Niall, Black Knee. The senior branch of this sept, the O'Neills of Tyrone, were frequently High Kings of Ireland and in the 16th century they were the leaders of the Gaelic resistance to English attempts to pacify Ireland. A junior branch established themselves in County Antrim in the 14th century and from their seat at Shane's Castle became known as the Clandeboy O'Neills.

O'Reilly (24) *Irish.* This powerful sept were chiefs of the ancient territory of Breffny which comprised Cavan and West Leitrim. At the height of their power in the Middle Ages their influence extended into Meath and Westmeath.

Organ (1) *English.* Derived from an occupational name for a player of a musical instrument. *Irish.* A South Tipperary variant of Horgan (See Hargan).

O'Rourke (1) *Irish.* This sept contested with the O'Reillys for the chieftainship of the ancient territory of Breffny. In the 10th century Breffny was divided into Breffny O'Rourke and Breffny O'Reilly which in the 16th century formed the basis for Counties Leitrim and Cavan respectively.

Orr (34) *Scottish.* Derived from the place name of Orr in Kirkcudbrightshire. It may also be an anglicisation of McIvor (See McIvor).

Osborne (1) *English* and *Scottish.* Derived from an Old Norse personal name which was established in England before the Norman Conquest of 1066. The surname was first recorded in Ireland in Counties Waterford and Tipperary in about 1550.

Osborough (1) *English.* It may be derived from a local name meaning Os's fort. Os could represent a shortened form of any number of Old English and Norse personal names which began Os or As, meaning god, e.g. Osborne (See Osborne).

Osbourne (1) See Osborne.

O'Somachain (1) *Irish.* This is the gaelic form of the County Sligo sept name of Somahan which was further anglicised to Somers and Summers.

Osuere (1) Originating from Warri in the State of Bendel in Nigeria this name came to Ireland in 1978.

O'Sullivan (4) *Irish.* Originating in South Tipperary this sept was forced westwards by the Norman invaders into Counties Cork and Kerry in the 13th century.

O'Toole (2) *Irish.* This sept which originated in County Kildare migrated to County Wicklow in the late 12th century in the face of Norman incursions.

Owens (12) A variant of both McKeown (See McKeown) and of O'Keown. The County Fermanagh sept of O'Keown were hereditary tenants of the church lands of Enniskillen. Some Owens may be of Welsh origin, simply meaning son of Owen.

P

Page (7) *English* and *Scottish.* Derived from an occupational name for a young servant. Recorded in Ireland since the 16th century Page has been gaelicised to McGill (See McGill).

Paige (1) A variant of Page. See Page.

Palin (1) *Welsh.* Derived from the Old Welsh personal name of Heilyn which originally denoted a "minister, serving at table". The Welsh prefix ap was reduced to p thus Palin means son of Heilyn. Cromwellian adventurers of this name were recorded in Dublin from the mid-17th century.

Panesar (1) Originating from the Sikh community in Northern India this name came to Derry in 1975.

Parfimowicz (1) This name is Polish in origin as the ending -owicz denotes son of.

Park (4) *English* and *Scottish*. Derived from a local name for someone who lived in a park or enclosure of thinly wooded land. It can also be an abbreviation of Parker (See Parker). In Scotland the surname was also derived from the lands of Park in Renfrewshire.

Parke (11) See Park.

Parker (3) *English* and *Scottish*. Derived from an occupational name for a park-keeper it was first recorded as a surname in Scotland in Perthshire in the 13th century.

Parkes (1) *English*. This variant of Park (See Park) is largely confined to Warwickshire and Worcestershire.

Parkhill (15) *Scottish*. Derived from the lands of Parkhill in Ayrshire it was recorded as a surname in Glasgow in 1605.

Parkhouse (1) *English*. Derived from a local name for someone who lived in a warden's lodge in a park. In the Middle Ages a park was a large enclosed area where the landowner could hunt game.

Parlour (1) *English*. Recorded as a surname in the Domesday Book of 1086 it probably derived as an occupational name for a servant who attended the parlour. It stems from the Old French word Parleur which was a room in a monastery for receiving guests.

Parsons (2) *English*. Derived either as an occupational name for the servant of a parish priest or as a nickname for the child of a parson. A family of this name settled at Birr, which was formerly known as Parsonstown, in County Offaly at the end of the 16th century. Irish McParson and Scottish McPherson (See McPherson) were sometimes abbreviated to Parsons.

Partridge (3) *English*. Derived either as a nickname from the bird or as an occupational name for a hunter of partridges. The surname was introduced to Ireland during the Cromwellian settlement of the mid-17th century. In some cases it was changed to Patrick.

Paterson (1) See Patterson.

Patterson (14) *Scottish*. Meaning son of Patrick this name originated in the Lowlands of Scotland. In the Highlands the sept name of McPatrick, meaning son of the devotee of Patrick, was anglicised to Patterson. McFetridge was also anglicised to Patterson (See

McFetridge). In Ireland the County Mayo sept name of McPadden was in some cases anglicised to Patterson.

Patton (13) Can be of *English, Scottish* or *Irish* origin. In England and Scotland Patton was variously derived from the personal name Patrick; from the place names of Patton in Shropshire and Westmorland; and from an occupational name for a clog maker. In Ireland the County Donegal sept of O'Pettane was anglicised to Patton.

Payne (5) *English.* Derived from the English given name Pain which was a popular name in the early Middle Ages. Recorded in Ireland since the 14th century this surname, by the 16th century, had given rise to six places in Southeast Ireland called Payneston.

Paynter (1) *English.* Derived from the occupational name for a painter.

Peacock (1) *English* and *Scottish.* Derived as a nickname for a vain, strutting person or for a 'dandy' it was recorded as a surname in the Domesday Book of 1086. Peacock was recorded in County Meath from the early 15th century.

Pears (1) *English.* This variant of Pearce (See Pierce) is chiefly found in Cornwall.

Pearson (4) *English* and *Scottish.* Meaning son of Piers (See Pierce) this surname was introduced to Ireland in the 17th century. In some cases Scottish McPherson (See McPherson) was shortened to Pearson.

Pedersen (1) A common surname in Norway and Denmark. The bearer of this name was born in Sunde I Sunnhordland in Norway and arrived in Derry in 1961. His grandfather was known as Peder Sunde and his descendants adopted the surname Pedersen which simply meant son of Peter. Thus in this particular case Pedersen has only been an hereditary surname for two generations.

Pegg (1) *English.* Derived from an occupational name for a maker of wooden pegs. It may, in a few cases, have originated as a nickname for a person with a wooden leg.

Pemberton (1) *English.* Derived from a Lancashire place name meaning barley settlement by the hill.

Pemble (1) The bearer of this name is of *English* origin. The first element may be derived from Welsh Pen meaning hill.

Peoples (27) *Irish*. The East Donegal and West Derry sept name of Deeny was usually mistranslated to Peoples. Both Peoples, also spelt Peebles, and Deeny are mainly found in the Raphoe area. In England Peoples is a variant of Pepys.

Percival (1) *English*. Derived from the personal name Perceval which was popularised by this Knight's quest for the holy grail in the 6th century legendary exploits of King Arthur and his Round Table.

Pettersen (1) Meaning son of Peter this name will be *Norwegian* in origin as the suffix sen was used there to denote son of (See Pedersen).

Petticrew (1) *Scottish*. Derived from a Norman nickname for a 'small man' this surname was recorded in Lanarkshire from the late 13th century. The name first came to Ulster, however, in the 17th century with one of the Huguenot families who settled in County Tyrone. (See Morrin).

Petropoulos The bearer of this name came from Cyprus.

Pewtner (3) Originating from Newport in Monmouthshire, Wales the original bearer of this name came to Ireland in the 1920s and married a Dublin girl before settling in Derry.

Phelan (5) *Irish*. This sept were Princes of Decies, an ancient territory covering West Waterford, before the 12th century Norman invasion. A branch of the sept also settled in Southwest Kilkenny. A small but distinct bardic sept of Phelan originated in West Ulster.

Phillips (6) Can be of *English*, *Scottish* or *Irish* origin. Meaning son of Philip this surname became very popular throughout England and the Lowlands of Scotland. In the Highlands of Scotland the sept name of McKillop was anglicised to Phillips. In Ireland the County Mayo sept of Philbin anglicised their name to Phillips.

Philson (6) *English*. This name simply means son of Philip (See Phillips).

Pickard (1) *English* and *Scottish*. Derived as a regional name for someone from Picardy in Northern France it was recorded as a surname in Scotland from the mid-13th century.

Pickett (1) *English* and *Scottish*. Derived from the Old French given name Picot this surname, which was recorded in the Domesday Book of 1086, was also spelt Piggott.

Pierce (2) *English.* Derived from the given name Piers which in turn was derived from the very popular medieval name of Peter. A family called Piers was granted lands in Westmeath in 1566. The Pierces or McPierces of Kerry were a branch of the Norman Fitzmaurices.

Pike (1) *English.* There are seven known derivations of this name including: a local name for someone who lived near a hill; an occupational name for a medieval foot soldier who used a pike; and a nickname for a tall, thin person. The surname was first recorded in Ireland at Youghal, County Cork in 1393. In a few cases Pike may be a variant of McPeake (See McPeake).

Pinkerton (1) *Scottish.* Derived from the lands of Pinkerton in East Lothian it was recorded as a surname there from the late 13th century.

Pinkett (1) *English.* A variant of Pinch which derived as a nickname for a 'chirpy person'.

Pitcaithley (1) *Scottish.* Derived from the Perthshire place name of Pitcaithly it was recorded as a surname there from the early 13th century.

Platt (4) *English.* Derived as a nickname for 'a thin man'. In Lancashire, in particular, Platt originated as a local name for someone who lived on a piece of flat land or by a plank-bridge.

Platts (1) See Platt.

Plews (4) *English.* Derived as an occupational name for a maker of ploughs.

Plummer (2) *English* and *Scottish.* Derived originally as an occupational name for a worker in lead. In a few cases it derived as a local name for someone who lived near a plum tree.

Podmore (1) *English.* Derived either from the Staffordshire place name of Podmore or from the Somerset place name of Podimore.

Pol (1) This name originated in Holland as a local name for someone who lived by a grassy mound. It may also have derived from the forename Paul.

Pollard (1) *English* and *Scottish.* Derived as a nickname for a person with close-cropped hair. It may also be derived from the forename Paul. A family of this name settled in County Westmeath in the 14th century at Castlepollard.

Pollock (8) *Scottish.* Derived from the lands of Upper Pollock in Renfrewhire. The family granted these lands in the 12th century adopted it as their surname. The name then spread throughout the Lowlands before coming to Ulster with the 17th century plantation.

Polwin (1) *English.* Tradition claims this old Cornish surname from the area of St. Blazey means white pool which refers to the whitepools left behind when china clay is mined using high-pressure water hoses.

Pomeroy (2) *English.* Derived from a number of place names in Northeast France meaning apple orchard. The Pomeroys established themselves in Devon in the 11th century and a branch of this family came to Ireland with the Earl of Essex in 1573.

Ponsomby (1) *English.* Derived from the Cumberland place name of Ponsonby meaning Puncun's settlement. The Ponsonbys accompanied Cromwell to Ireland in the mid-17th century and acquired large estates in Counties Kerry and Kilkenny.

Poole (1) *English.* Derived from a local name for someone who lived near a pool or pond.

Porteous (1) *Scottish.* It may be derived from a local name for someone who lived in the lodge at the entrance to a manor house. Chiefly found in the Scottish Borders the surname first came to Ireland in the person of an army officer who was recorded in 1563 in County Leix.

Porter (38) *English* and *Scottish.* This occupational name can have three meanings, the most likely one being a doorkeeper. In the Middle Ages the office of porter was a very important one in both castle and monastery. In some cases Porter referred to a person who could be hired to carry baggage while in Scotland it had an additional meaning of ferryman. Porter was first recorded in Ireland in the 13th century.

Potts (2) *English.* Meaning son of Philpott this surname was ultimately derived from Philip (See Phillips).

Power (7) *English.* Derived from Old French Pohier meaning a native of Picardy it was introduced to Ireland, at the time of the Anglo-Norman invasion of the 12th century, as le Poer. Through time

Power came to be regarded as a great gaelic name especially in County Waterford and adjoining counties.

Poyntz (1) *English.* Derived from the medieval given name Pons which in turn derived from Roman Pontius. The surname was first recorded in Ireland with Hugh Poyntz who served there in 1210. Poyntz was recorded in Armagh from the 17th century.

Prasad (1) There are four references to Prasad in Irish telephone directories, of which two occur in Northern Ireland.

Preston (1) *English* and *Scottish.* Derived from a number of Northern English place names, the most notable one in Lancashire, meaning village with a priest. In Scotland the surname was also derived from the lands of Preston in Midlothian. Prestons from Lancashire came to Ireland in 1270 and acquired estates in Counties Dublin and Meath. During the 17th century rebellions they fought on the Irish side.

Price (3) *Welsh.* Meaning son of Rhys this is one of the commonest Welsh surnames. It has been recorded in Ireland since the 14th century. In some cases Price is a variant of Bryson (See Bryson). Price may also be an English surname derived from Old French Pris meaning price or prize.

Priestley (2) *English.* Derived from a number of place names, especially the one in North Yorkshire, meaning a wood or clearing belonging to the church.

Prince (1) *English.* Derived from a nickname denoting someone who behaved in a princely manner it was recorded as a surname in Edinburgh in the late 17th century.

Proctor (2) *English* and *Scottish.* Derived from the occupational name for a steward the term was used most commonly for an attorney in a church court. Families of this name settled in Counties Armagh and Donegal in the mid-17th century.

Pulis (1) In all of Ireland the only reference to Pulis in the telephone directories is in Derry.

Purdy (2) *English* and *Scottish.* Derived from a nickname for someone who frequently made use of the oath 'pour dieu' i.e. by God. This name, usually spelt Purdie, was recorded in Scotland from the late 13th century.

Pyke (1) See Pike.

Pyne (4) *English.* Derived from a local name for someone who lived in a pine forest. The earliest reference to this name in Ireland is 1599. Families of this name have been located mainly in County Cork with a few in Clare.

Pyper (2) *English* and *Scottish.* Derived from the occupational name for a piper. In Scotland Pyper was a common name in Perth from an early date.

Pywell (1) Probably of *English* origin this name is only recorded in Derry in the Northern Ireland phone book. Well is a very common element in English place names meaning well, spring or stream. Py could possibly be derived from Old French Pie meaning insect. Thus Pywell may be derived from an English place name meaning stream infested by insects.

Q

Quieley (1) A variant of Queally (See Kealey). Much confusion has arisen between Kealy, Keeley, Kiely, Keily and Queally.

Quigg (12) *Irish.* Originating as a sept in County Derry this name is chiefly found in this county. It can also be a shortened form of Quigley (See Quigley).

Quigley (68) *Irish.* By the end of the 16th century this sept, which originated in County Mayo, had become dispersed with its main concentration located in Counites Derry and Donegal. A sept called Quigley also originated in the Inishowen Peninsula, County Donegal.

Quinlan (1) *Irish.* Tracing their descent from the 5th century Niall of the Nine Hostages this sept, which originated in County Meath, usually anglicised its name to Kindellan and at a later date to Connellan and Conlan. A branch also settled in North Tipperary but they anglicised their name to Quinlan.

Quinn (1) *Irish.* This County Tyrone sept, which traces its descent from Eoghan, son of the 5th century Niall of the Nine Hostages, acted as quartermasters to the O'Neills.

R

Rabbett (5) *Irish.* This name is usually a mistranslation of the gaelic sept name of Kinneen or Cunneen. Three distinct septs of this name originated in Counties Clare, Mayo and Offaly. In England Rabbitt derived from the personal names of both Robert and French Radbode.

Radcliffe (4) *English.* Chiefly found in Lancashire this name derived from a number of place names meaning red cliff or riverbank.

Rafferty (8) *Irish.* Septs of this name originated in Counties Donegal and Sligo. The name has become confused with O'Roarty. The O'Roartys were abbots to St. Columba on Tory Island off the coast of Donegal.

Rainey (7) *English* and *Scottish.* Derived from the Old German personal name Reginald which was introduced to England by the Normans. In Scotland a family of this name owned extensive lands in Angus from the mid-15th century.

Ralphs (1) *English* and *Scottish.* Meaning son of Ralph this surname was derived from the Old Norse personal name of Radwolf which was introduced into England by Scandinavian settlers. In the town of Nairn in Scotland Ralph and other surnames of Norse origin can be found.

Ramsay (5) See Ramsey.

Ramsey (19) *English* and *Scottish.* Derived from the place name Ramsay found in both Huntingdonshire and Essex. In Scotland Ramsays of Anglo-Norman origin acquired lands in Lothian in the 12th century. A century later they were landowners in Angus and as a clan they were beginning to figure prominently in the Border wars.

Rankin (14) *Scots Gaelic.* In Counties Derry and Donegal Rankins trace their descent from an Argyllshire sept of Clan MacLean. The McRankins of Glencoe, meaning son of Francis, were hereditary pipers to the MacLeans. These Rankins were quite distinct from the Lowland Rankins, who were particularly common in Ayrshire, and who derived their surname from the personal name Randolph.

Ravindran Originating from the State of Kerala in Southwest India this name came to Derry in 1988.

Rawdon (1) *English.* Derived from the West Riding of Yorkshire place name meaning red hill.

Rea (2) Can be of *English, Scottish* or *Irish* origin. The most probable origin of the name in the Derry area is as an abbreviated form of McCrae (See McCrae). The name also originated in Dumfriesshire as early as the 13th century. In England Rea derived as a local name for someone who lived by a stream while in Ulster names such as O'Rawe and Reagh were anglicised to Rea. Today Rea has become confused with Wray (See Wray).

Redden (5) *Irish.* This County Clare sept were hereditary stewards to the O'Briens.

Reddin (1) See Redden.

Reed (1) See Reid.

Regan (1) *Irish.* There were three septs of this name: In County Leix the Regans were one of the Tribes of Tara; in Clare they were a branch of the O'Briens; and in Cork they were a branch of the McCarthys.

Rehill (1) *Irish.* Originating in County Fermanagh known variants of this name include Reighill, Rahill and Reckle.

Reid (19) Can be of *English, Scottish* or *Irish* origin. In England and Scotland it was, in most cases, derived from a nickname meaning 'red', as in red hair or ruddy complexion. Some derived their name from various place names. In Scotland the Reids were one of the lesser riding clans of the Scottish Borders. Furthermore the Highland septs of McRory and McInroy were anglicised to Reid. In Ireland the County Mayo sept of Mulderrig anglicised its name to Reid.

Reidy (1) *Irish.* Originating in County Tipperary this sept migrated westwards and settled in Counties Clare and Kerry.

Reilly (6) See O'Reilly.

Renshaw (2) *English.* Derived from the Derbyshire place name meaning Reynold's copse. This surname is chiefly found in Derbyshire, South Yorkshire and Lancashire.

Reynolds (2) Can be of *English, Scottish* or *Irish* origin. Meaning son of Reynold this name, derived from the Old German personal name Reginald, was introduced to Britain by the Normans. The Scots Gaelic sept name of McRanald and the County Leitrim sept name of McRannall were anglicised to McReynolds and Reynolds.

Rhodes (1) *English.* Chiefly found in Yorkshire this name was derived from a local name for someone who lived in a clearing in woodland.

Richardson (1) *English* and *Scottish.* Meaning son of Richard this name, derived from the Old German personal name Ricard, ws introduced to England by the Normans. The name was first recorded in Scotland in Lanarkshire in the early 14th century.

Richmond (5) *English* and *Scottish.* Derived from a number of place names found in Northern France and England, the most notable one in North Yorkshire, meaning rich hill. Richmond was recorded as a surname in Scotland from the early 17th century.

Riddles (5) *English* and *Scottish.* Derived either from the North Yorkshire regional name of Ryedale meaning the valley of the River Rye or from the Norman personal name Ridel. The Riddells established themselves in Roxburghshire, Scotland from the mid-12th century.

Rigby (1) *English.* Derived from the Lancashire place name meaning ridge settlement.

Rigney (1) *Irish.* This sept originated in Garrycastle, County Offaly. In County Mayo especially Rigney was anglicised to Reaney.

Ringland (1) *English.* Derived from the Norfolk place name of Ringland. Land is a common second element in English place names, usually meaning estate. The first element Ring, in this case, was a tribal name whose original form has become obscured.

Ritchie (4) *Scottish.* Derived from the personal name Richard (See Richardson) the Ritchies were a sept of Clan Mackintosh in Perthshire.

Riviere (1) Derived from a number of place names in Northern France called Rivieres, meaning rivers. A Huguenot family named Riviere settled in England around 1689 (See Morrin).

Robb (11) *Scottish.* Derived from the Old English personal name Robert this name was originally McRobb. In addition to being a sept of the Stewarts of Appin in Argyll the McRobbs were septs of Clans Buchanan and MacFarlane.

Roberts (11) *English* and *Scottish.* Derived from the popular Old English personal name Robert this name, together with Robertson, became more common in Scotland than in England. In Perthshire Clan Robertson took its name from their 15th century chief, Grizzled Robert. Clan Robertson was also known as Clan Donnachie. After the 1745 Jacobite Rising many Robertsons adopted the name Donachie which was further anglicised to Duncan (See Duncan).

Robertson (1) See Roberts and Robinson.

Robinson (38) Derived originally from the personal name Robert (See Roberts) Robinson is generally regarded as an English name and Robertson as a Scottish one. In Ulster, however, Robertson and Robinson have lost this neat distinction.

Robison (1) See Roberts and Robinson.

Robson (2) *English* and *Scottish.* Meaning son of Robert (See Roberts) this surname is chiefly found in Northumberland. The Robsons were also recorded in the Scottish Borders from the mid-15th century.

Roche (1) *English.* Originating as de la Roche (of the rock) in France this name came to Ireland at the time of the Anglo-Norman invasion in the 12th century. Settling in Cork and Wexford Roche came to be regarded as a great Gaelic Irish sept. There are 16 places called Rochestown in Ireland.

Rodden (3) See McCrudden.

Roddy (18) *Irish.* There were two distinct septs of this name; one originating in County Leitrim and the other in Donegal. The latter were hereditary tenants of the church lands at Taughboyne. In some cases Roddy has become confused with the County Kilkenny sept name of Reddy.

Rodger (1) See Rodgers.

Rodgers (16) Can be of *English, Scottish* or *Irish* origin. Derived from the Germanic personal name Roger this surname, meaning son of Rodger, was introduced to Britain by the Normans. In Ireland McGrory (See McGrory) and its variants such as McRory were anglicised to Rodgers.

Rogan (1) *Irish.* Originating in the ancient territory of Oriel this sept was of considerable importance in Armagh and West Down up to the end of the 12th century.

Rogers (1) See Rodgers.

Rolston (1) See Roulston.

Rooney (10) *Irish.* This County Down sept, with its homeland near Rathfriland, was noted, from the 11th century, for their literary prowess. Furthermore the County Fermanagh sept of Mulrooney, Kings of Fermanagh before the Maguires, had their name shortened to Rooney.

Rosborough (8) *Scottish.* Derived from the town of Roxburgh in the Scottish Borders this surname was well established, as Rosebrough and Rosebrugh, in the Claudy/Banagher area of County Derry by 1796. In 1831 Rosboroughs were concentrated in the parishes of Cumber and Banagher and Roxboroughs in Aghadowey Parish.

Ross (18) *English* and *Scottish.* Derived from various place names found throughout England. A Yorkshire family of the name settled in Ayrshire in the 12th century; a branch of whom, in turn, settled in County Down in the 17th century. In the North of Scotland Clan Ross, with origins in the 13th century, took their name from the ancient Province of Ross.

Rossborough (2) See Rosborough.

Roulston (9) *English.* Derived from various place names found throughout England, meaning Rolf's farm.

Row (2) Can be of *English, Scottish* or *Irish* origin. In England it was derived from local names for someone who either lived in a row of houses or by rough, uncultivated ground. In Scotland it was derived from the Dunbartonshire place name of Row. In Ireland the epithet Ruadh (meaning red) was turned into the surname Roe or Rowe from the 17th century by English administrators with no knowledge of gaelic. In addition the Waterford sept name of Ormond was anglicised to Roe while the Cavan/Leitrim sept name of McEnroe was shortened to Roe.

Rowan (4) *Irish.* The County Galway and County Mayo sept names of Ruane, the County Clare name of Roughans and the East Clare name of Rohan were further anglicised to Rowan. *Scottish.* Derived from the Scottish pronounciation of Rolland (See Rowland) this surname was recorded in Aberdeen and Glasgow from the early 16th century.

Rowe (2) See Row.

Rowland (1) *English* and *Scottish.* Derived either from the Norman personal name Rolant or from place names in Derbyshire and Sussex meaning roe deer wood. *Irish.* Originating in County Mayo this sept, whose base was on the eastern side of the River Easkey, County Sligo, anglicised their name to Rowley and Rowland.

Royan (1) *Irish.* A variant of Ruane (See Rowan). In County Mayo especially Royan was changed to Ryan (See Mulrine).

Royle (1) *English.* Chiefly found in Lancashire this surname was derived from the Lancashire place name meaning roe deer hill.

Rudd (2) *English.* Derived from a nickname for a person with red hair or a ruddy complexion this surname came to Ireland in the first half of the 17th century.

Ruddock (2) *English.* Derived from a nickname from the bird, the robin-red-breast, this surname was recorded in Dumfries, Scotland in the late 17th century.

Rush (3) *Irish.* By the 17th century a sept of this name was well established in Counties Armagh and Monaghan. In addition the County Sligo sept name of Loughry was frequently translated to Rush. *English.* Derived from a local name for someone who lived near a clump of rushes.

Rushe (1) See Rush.

Russell (12) *English* and *Scottish.* Derived from a nickname meaning 'red' this surname became quite widespread all over England and Scotland. In the Scottish Highlands the Russells were septs of Clan Buchanan and Cumming. A Norman family of the name came to County Down in the 12th century.

Rutherford (17) *Scottish.* Derived from the place name in Roxburghshire meaning ford of the horned cattle. On record since the 12th century the Rutherfords became one of the most powerful riding clans of the Scottish Borders.

Rutledge (1) *Scottish.* Derived from a place name which can no longer be identified the Rutledges were based in the Scottish Borders where they were one of the lesser riding clans.

Ryan (7) See Mulrine.

S

Saint (2) *English.* Derived as a nickname for a pious individual.

Sala (1) An Italian variant of the English name Sale which derived as an occupational name for someone who was employed at the manor house.

Salter (1) *English* and *Scottish.* Derived as an occupational name for a dealer in salt it was recorded in Scotland from the mid-15th century. Salt was a precious commodity in medieval times, used to both preserve and season food.

Salvesen (1) Borne by an United States Service man who came to serve in the American Base in Derry in the late 1940s this surname was originally *Norwegian* in origin.

Sammon (5) *Irish.* A recorded variant of Salmon which in turn was an anglicisation of the sept name of Bradden which can be found in Counties Donegal and Leitrim. *English.* Derived from the Old French given name Salomon families of this name settled in Counties Kildare and Dublin in the ealy 16th century.

Sanderson (1) *English* and *Scottish.* Derived from the medieval given name Sander which in turn was derived from the forename Alexander it was recorded in Kincardineshire, Scotland from the early 15th century.

Sands (2) *English* and *Scottish.* In England the name was originally spelt Sandys and it denoted someone who lived on sandy soil or by a beach. In Scotland the name was derived from the lands of Sands in Fifeshire where it is on record as a surname since the 15th century.

Sandy (1) *English.* Derived either from the Bedfordshire place name meaning sand island or from the Old Norse personal name of Sand.

Sargent (1) *English* and *Scottish.* Derived from the occupational name for a servant it can be found frequently in medieval Irish records.

Sargent is now a common name in County Armagh.

Saunders (1) Meaning son of Sanders it is another form of Sanderson (See Sanderson).

Savage (1) *English.* Derived from a nickname meaning 'savage' or 'wild' the Savages accompanied William the Conqueror to England in 1066. In the 12th century they took part in the Anglo-Norman invasion of Ireland and were granted territory in the Ards Peninsula, County Down.

Saville (1) *English.* Derived from the place name of Sainville in Northern France meaning Saxon settlement.

Sayers (2) *English.* Chiefly found in Sussex and meaning son of Sayer there are six known derivations of this name. It may be derived from the personal name Seir or from the occupational name sawyer.

Scallon (2) *Irish.* The sept name of Scallan was formerly very numerous in Wexford. In Fermanagh Scullion (See Scullion) has been made Scallan.

Scampton (1) *English.* Derived from the Lincolnshire place name meaning either short settlement or Skammi's settlement. The first element in this name is of Norse origin.

Scanlon (1) *Irish.* There were several septs of this name, the most important originating in County Cork. The County Sligo name of Scannell was made Scanlan in Counties Donegal and Sligo.

Scarlett (2) *English* and *Scottish.* Derived from the occupational name for a dyer or seller of rich, bright fabrics a family of this name held lands in Caithness, Scotland from the 14th century.

Scheel (1) Originating in Germany and arriving in Derry in 1973 this surname is a variant of Schiller which derived as a nickname for a person with a squint.

Schenkel (1) Originating from Vienna, Austria this Jewish family settled in Derry in 1938 where they set up business in Bigger's Stores on Foyle Street.

Schlindwein (2) Originating in the town of Baden-Baden in Bavaria in West Germany the original bearer of the name arrived here via Germantown, Philadelphia, U.S.A. in 1891. On emigrating to Philadelphia he married a Derry girl and from here he came to Derry with his wife and 2-year-old son. The name seems to contain two elements; Schlein meaning Tench (which was a freshwater fish) and Wein meaning wine. Ornamental surnames such as these were adopted by the Jewish community in Europe when they began to adopt surnames at the beginning of the 19th century.

Schmid (1) *German.* Derived as an occupational name for a worker in metal. As well as making horseshoes and ploughshares medieval smiths forged swords and armour.

Scholes (1) *English.* Derived from a local name in Northern England for someone who lived in a rough hut or shed it was recorded as a surname in County Limerick from the 14th century.

Scoltock (2) Introduced to Derry by an Englishman family tradition claims that the name was Scandinavian in origin. It may also be a variant of Scottish Scoloc which derived as a term for the lowest members of the order in a medieval Celtic monastic community. In return for scoloc or scholar lands the tenant was bound to supply clerks, who could read and write, to the monastery.

Scott (17) *Scottish.* The term Scot originally referred to the gaelic colonists from Eastern Ulster (See McNally) who had established themselves in Kintyre and Argyll by the beginning of the 6th century. The Scotts, who acquired their lands in the 12th century, became one of the most powerful riding clans in the Scottish Borders who at the height of their power in the 16th century could muster an army of 600 men.

Scroggie (1) *Scottish.* Derived from the village of Scroggie in Perthshire this name is most common in the Ballymena area.

Scruton (1) *English.* Derived from a North Yorkshire place name meaning Skurfa's settlement. Skurfa was an Old Norse byname.

Scullion (1) *Irish.* This sept were hereditary tenants of the church lands of Ballyscullion in County Derry.

Seaton (1) *English* and *Scottish.* Derived from a number of place names, mostly found in Northern England, meaning sea or lake settlement. In Scotland a powerful Norman family of the name acquired lands in East Lothian in the 12th century.

Seeley (1) *English.* Derived from a nickname for a person with a cheeful disposition.

Selby (1) *English.* Derived from a West Yorkshire place name meaning willow farm this surname is now very common in Nottinghamshire.

Semple (11) *English* and *Scottish.* Derived from a number of place names in Normandy called Saint-Paul, from the dedication of their churches to St. Paul. A Scottish family of this name held the hereditary post of Sheriff of Renfrewshire from the 13th century.

Shamsuddin (1) In all of Ireland the only reference to Shamsuddin in the telephone directories is in Derry.

Shanagher (1) *Irish.* Little is known about this sept name except that it is chiefly found in County Roscommon.

Shanks (1) *English.* Derived as a nickname for someone with 'long legs' this surname was especially common in Northumberland. *Scottish.* Derived from the lands of Shank in Midlothian. The family granted these lands adopted it as their surname in the late 13th century.

Shannon (2) *Irish.* Various septs including Shanahan, Shinane and Giltenan of County Clare anglicised their name to Shannon. By the 14th century some of the name had settled in Scotland in Galloway and Kintyre. In Kintyre the Shannons became harpers to the MacDonalds.

Sharkey (19) *Irish.* This sept originated in County Tyrone as O'Sharkey but the prefix O was dropped by the 18th century.

Sharp (2) Can be of *English, Scottish* or *Irish* origin. In England and Scotland it derived as a nickname for 'a sharp, smart person'. It was recorded as a surname in Dumfries, Scotland in the late 14th century. In County Donegal the Mayo sept name of Guerin was anglicised to Sharpe.

Sharpe (1) See Sharp.

Shaw (6) *English* and *Scottish.* In England it derived as a local name for someone who lived by a wood. In Lowland Scotland it was derived from a number of places of the name while in the Highlands Clan Shaw, one of the principal clans of the confederation of Clan Chattan, originated as a branch of Clan Mackintosh. The name became common in Ulster with the 17th century plantation.

Sheehan (3) *Irish.* Originating in County Limerick this large sept spread southwards into Counties Cork and Kerry. In the Middle

Ages a minor sept of the name were hereditary trumpeters to the O'Kellys of Galway.

Sheehy (1) *Scots Gaelic.* As a branch of Clan MacDonnell the Sheehys first came to County Limerick in the early 15th century as galloglasses (mercenary soldiers).

Sheenan (1) *Irish.* This County Tyrone sept name has to some extent been absorbed by Shannon in County Monaghan (See Shannon).

Sheeran (1) See Sheerin.

Sheerin (13) *Irish.* There were two distinct septs of this name; one originating in Cork and the other in the Donegal/Fermanagh area. The former is now extinct while the latter spread as far south as County Leix.

Sheils (1) See Shields.

Shephard (1) *English* and *Scottish.* Derived from the occupational name for a shepherd it was first recorded in Ireland in Counties Dublin and Kildare in the 13th century.

Sheppard (1) See Shephard.

Sheridan (3) *Irish.* Originating in County Longford as hereditary tenants of church lands there they later migrated to County Cavan where they became followers of the O'Reillys.

Sherin (1) See Sheerin.

Sherrard (5) *English.* Of uncertain derivation this name has been closely associated with Derry since the 17th century. Two Sherrards were among the thirteen apprentices who closed the gates of Derry in the face of James II's army in December 1688.

Shields (14) Can be of *English, Scottish* or *Irish* origin. In England and Scotland it derived either from a local name for someone who lived by a shelter or shallow place or from an occupational name for a maker of shields. In Ireland the Shiels or Shields, with origins in Inishowen, County Donegal and tracing their descent from the 5th century Niall of the Nine Hostages, were a sept of hereditary physicians. In Derry most Shields and Shiels will be of this origin.

Shiels (15) See Shields.

Shirley (1) *English.* Derived from a number of place names meaning bright wood this name was recorded in Scotland as Sherlaw from the late 14th century.

Short (2) *Irish.* Some McGirrs (See McGirr) anglicised their name to Short. *English* and *Scottish.* Derived from a nickname which referred to the shortness in height of the original bearer it was recorded in Scotland from the early 15th century.

Shortt (1) See Short.

Shotter (1) *English.* Chiefly found in East Midlands it derived as an occupational name for a marksman i.e. a shooter or an archer.

Shuter (1) A variant of Shotter. See Shotter.

Siddiqui (1) Originating in Saudi Arabia it became a common surname in the Indo-Pakistan sub-continent. The bearer of this name arrived in Northern Ireland from Karachi in Pakistan in 1971.

Sidebottom (2) *English.* Derived from a Cheshire place name meaning wide valley.

Sidwell (1) *English.* Derived from a now unidentified place name in Northern England, perhaps meaning stream in a deep valley.

Simmonds (1) Meaning son of Simmond this name derived as another form of Simon (See Simpson).

Simmons (1) A variant of Simmonds. See Simmonds.

Simms (6) Meaning son of Simon this name has the same origins as Simpson (See Simpson).

Simpkin (1) Meaning little Simon it has the same origins as Simpson (See Simpson).

Simpson (49) *English* and *Scottish.* Meaning son of Simon it was derived from the Old Testament name Simeon which became a very popular medieval first name. In Devon in the 13th century three places named Simpson gave rise to the surname there. In the Highlands of Scotland McKimmie, a sept of Clan Fraser, whose name meant son of Simon, was anglicised to Simpson. Simpson has been recorded in Ulster since the 17th century.

Sinclair (3) *Scottish.* This clan takes its name from St. Clair in Normandy. A family of this name of Norman origin obtained lands in Midlothian in the 12th century. They became Earls of Orkney in the 14th century and Earls of Caithness in the 15th century. Sinclair became a very common surname in Caithness and the Orkneys as the tenants on these lands adopted the name of their overlord.

Singh (6) Originating from the State of Punjab in Northern India this name, meaning lion warriors, came to Derry in 1954.

Siripurapu (1) The bearer of this name came to Ireland from India in 1934 to work as a doctor.

Skavan (1) Originating from Copenhagen in Denmark the bearer of this name came to Derry during the Second World War and married a local girl.

Skeet (4) *English.* Derived from the Old Norse byname of Skjotr meaning swift.

Skeffington (1) *English.* Derived from the Leicestershire place name meaning Sceaft's settlement it has been recorded in Ireland since the mid-16th century.

Skeggs (1) *English.* Meaning son of Skegg it is derived from the Old Norse byname Skegg meaning beard.

Skuce (1) *English.* Derived from a number of minor place names in Cornwall meaning elder bush.

Slater (1) *English* and *Scottish.* Derived from the occupational name for someone who covered roofs with slate it was recorded as Sclater in Aberdeen, Scotland in 1399. The name was introduced to Longford and Louth by Cromwellian settlers in the mid-17th century.

Slavin (1) *Irish.* Tracing their descent from Eoghan, son of the 5th century Niall of the Nine Hostages, this sept was an old ecclesiastical and bardic family in Fermanagh. By the 17th century a branch of the name had settled in Westmeath.

Slevin (6) A variant of Slavin. See Slavin.

Sloan (2) *Irish.* Two distinct septs with origins in Counties Down and Fermanagh anglicised their name to Sloan. By the early 16th century some of the name had established themselves in Scotland in Galloway; some of these returned to Ulster in the 17th century as planters.

Sloane (2) See Sloan.

Sluss (1) It may be a variant of Scottish Sloss which is an abbreviated form of Auchincloss which was derived from the lands of that name in Ayrshire. It may even be a variant of Dutch Sluis which derived as a local name for someone who lived by a lock or weir.

Smalls (1) Can be of *English, Scottish* or *Irish* origin. In England and

Scotland it derived from a nickname meaning 'small' or 'thin'. In Scotland it can also be a sept of Clan Murray. In Ireland Begg (See Beggs) was translated to Small while Kielty was mistranslated to Small.

Smallwood (3) *English.* Chiefly found in the Midlands this surname was derived either from the Cheshire place name meaning narrow wood or from a local name for someone who lived in a small wood.

Smallwoods (5) See Smallwood.

Smartt (1) *English* and *Scottish.* Derived from the nickname for an 'active person' it was recorded as a surname in Scotland from the late 14th century where Smert was the common pronounciation of the name.

Smellie (1) *Scottish.* Derived from a nickname for someone who had 'a strong body odour' it was recorded in Glasgow in the early 17th century.

Smith (33) Can be of *English, Scottish* or *Irish* origin. It is the commonest surname in England, Scotland, Wales and Ulster. This occupational name sprang up all over England wherever there was a smith. In Scotland and Ireland Smith was a further anglicisation of McGowan (See McGowan).

Smy (1) *English.* Originating from Suffolk the original bearer of this name came to Derry during the First World War as a merchant seaman and married a local girl.

Smyth (51) See Smith.

Smythe (2) See Smith.

Snodgrass (9) *Scottish.* This Ayrshire surname is derived from the lands of Snodgers or Snodgrasse in the parish of Irvine in Ayrshire. It was recorded as a surname in Ayr from the late 14th century.

Soal (3) *English.* Derived either as a local name for someone who lived near a muddy place or as a nickname for an 'unmarried man'.

Speer (5) *English* and *Scottish.* Derived either as a nickname for a notable thrower of the spear or as an occupational name for a watchman or spyer it was first recorded in Scotland in the early 13th century. The name was not much known in Ulster before the 18th century. In fact two of the early Speer settlers who came to County Derry from Scotland, namely David Spier and John Spear of

Coleraine emigrated through the port of Derry to North America in the years before 1725.

Speers (1) See Speer.

Spence (8) *English* and *Scottish.* Derived as an occupational name for the person in charge of the larder or provisions room. In Scotland the Spences were also a sept of Clan MacDuff and they were standard-bearers to the clan.

Spencer (2) A variant of Spence (See Spence). In addition the County Tipperary sept name of McSpillane was occasionally anglicised to Spenser.

Sperou (1) Originating from Famagusta in the Greek part of Cyprus this name came to Derry in 1963.

Spiers (2) See Speer.

Spratt (4) *English.* Derived from the nickname for 'a small person'.

Sproule (6) *Scottish.* Recorded from the 13th century in Dunbartonshire and Lanarkshire as Spreul this name has been established in Counties Derry and Donegal since the early 17th century.

Stafford (3) *English.* Derived from a number of place names, including the county town ot Staffordshire, meaning landing place ford. A powerful Anglo-Norman family of this name settled in County Wexford in the 13th century. In Ulster Gaelic McStocker was anglicised to Stafford from the 17th century.

Stainsby (1) *English.* Derived from place names in Derbyshire and Lincolnshire meaning respectively Steinn's and Stafn's settlements. The first elements in both names were Old Norse personal names.

Stanage (2) Recorded as both Stanage and Stannage this name is now common in Northern Ireland. Old English Stan, meaning stone (See Stone), is a common first element in English place names. For example Stoneage, recorded in Essex in the 14th century, derived as a local name for someone who lived near a stone gate.

Stanford (1) *English.* Derived from a great number of place names meaning stone ford.

Starrett (11) *Scottish.* Derived from the Ayrshire place name of Stairaird (now known as Stirie) this name, variously spelt as Stirrat and Starrat, was once very common in the parish of Dalry in

Ayrshire. In Ulster the name was spelt Starrett and Sterritt where it became well known in Donegal and adjacent areas. In a few cases it may be derived from English Start which was derived from a number of minor place names meaning a promontory.

Starrs (3) *English.* Derived from a nickname meaning 'star' a family of this name became established in North Tipperary during the Cromwellian settlement of the mid-17th century. Known as Starr in England it is better known in Ulster as Starrs.

Steele (2) *English* and *Scottish.* Derived from a nickname meaning 'steel', to denote firmness and reliability. In Scotland it was also derived from places of the name found in Ayrshire, Berwickshire and Dumfriesshire.

Stein (1) *Scottish.* This is a form of Steven (See Stevenson) found chiefly in Ayrshire, Fifeshire, the Lothians and the Borders.

Stelfox (1) This may possibly be a combination of the *English* names Stell and Fox (See Fox). Stell derived as a local name for someone who lived by a fish trap in a river.

Sterling (3) *Scottish.* Derived from the town of Stirling in Stirlingshire which was recorded as Strevelin in the 12th century.

Sterritt (3) See Starrett.

Stevenson (16) *English* and *Scottish.* Meaning son of Steven it was derived from the personal name Stephen which was popularised by the Normans. Stevenson is usually regarded as the Scottish form of the name and Stephenson as the English. But this distinction is now largely blurred. Steenson and Stinson are variants of the name found only in Ulster. The Stevensons who settled in the Lurgan area in County Armagh in the 17th century were quakers and/or linen weavers from England.

Stewart (49) *Scottish.* Derived from the Old English occupational name of Steward who was the keeper of a household. As every Bishop or Landlord had his Steward the name sprang up all over Scotland. From the 12th century Walter, the High Steward of the Royal household, who was responsible for the collection of taxes and the administration of justice, descended the Scottish Royal family of Stewart. Clan Stewart, which also traces its descent from the above Walter, later divided into separate clans: the Stewarts of

Appin; of Atholl; of Bute and of Galloway. Nine of the 59 Scottish undertakers granted lands in the 17th century plantation of Ulster were Stewarts.

Stewart-Liberty (1) A double-barrelled surname. See Stewart.

Stickley (1) In this case the name originated from London. As ley is a very common second element in English place names (meaning wood or clearing) it is possible that Stickley derived as a place name meaning Sticca's wood. It is also possible that Stickley is a variant of Scottish Stiklaw which was recorded in St. Andrews and Inverness in the 13th and 14th centuries.

Stokes (2) *English.* Derived from a great number of place names meaning place, which originated as a term for an outlying hamlet. It has been recorded in Ireland since the 14th century.

Stone (3) Can be of *English*, *Scottish* or *Irish* origin. In England it derived as a local name for someone who lived either by stony ground or by a notable outcrop of rock. The name was recorded in the Scottish Borders in the late 13th century while in Ireland the Connemara name of Clogherty and the Sligo name of Muckley were translated to Stone.

Stonell (1) *English.* It may be derived from the Staffordshire place name of Stonal meaning stony corner or from Stanhill which derived as a local name for someone who lived by a stony hill.

Stoneman (2) *English.* Derived either as a local name for someone who lived by the stone (See Stone) or as an occupational name for a stone mason.

Storey (3) *English* and *Scottish.* Derived from the Old Norse byname Stori meaning big it was recorded as a surname in Scotland from the late 13th century. Several families of the name settled in Ulster, especially in Tyrone, in the 17th century.

Stott (1) *English* and *Scottish.* Derived either as a nickname meaning 'steer' or as an occupational name for a keeper of bullocks. It was recorded as a surname in Aberdeen, Scotland in the late 15th century.

Strain (3) *Irish.* A County Down variant of the Donegal sept name of Strahan who were hereditary tenants of the church lands of Conwall. It may also be a variant of Scottish Strachan which derived its name from the lands of Strachan in Kincardineshire.

Strawbridge (10) This name is very much associated with the Derry area and is probably *Scottish* in origin. Recorded as Strobridge and Strawbridge in the 1663 Hearth Money Rolls in Templemore and Cumber parishes respectively this name has been associated with the rural parishes, especially Glendermot parish, to the east of Derry city for well over 300 years.

Street (3) *English.* Derived from a number of Southern English place names meaning Roman Road. It would have referred to places on or near Roman roads.

Strickland (1) *English.* Derived from the Cumberland place name meaning bullock land this name has been common in Lancashire from the early 14th century.

Stroud (1) *English.* Derived from place names in Gloucestershire and Middlesex meaning marshy ground overgrown with brushwood.

Strunks (1) This name of *German* origin is only recorded in Derry in the Northern Ireland phone book.

Struthers (3) *English* and *Scottish.* Derived either from a local name for damp land or from place names such as Struthers in Fifeshire, Struther in Lancashire or Strother in Northumberland.

Strutthers (1) See Struthers.

Stuart (3) This French spelling of Stewart (See Stewart) was made popular through the fame of Mary Queen of Scots.

Stuiver (1) The bearer of this name came to Derry from Holland in 1961.

Sturgeon (1) *English* and *Scottish.* Derived from an occupational name for a fishmonger. In Scotland the name was largely confined to Dumfriesshire and Kirkcudbrightshire where it was recorded from the mid-16th century.

Sumra (2) Originating from the State of Punjab in Northern India this name came to Derry in 1938.

Sutherland (3) *Scottish.* Derived from the county name of Sutherland this clan acquired its extensive territory in the early 13th century. The Sutherlands feuded frequently with their neighbours, especially with the Mackeys.

Swain (1) *English* and *Scottish.* Derived either from the Old Norse personal name of Sveinn or from the occupational name for a servant. It was recorded in Leinster from 1288. It is claimed that in some cases Sweeney (See Sweeney) was changed to Swain. Swain has also become confused with Swan (See Swann).

Swann (2) *English* and *Scottish*. Derived either as a variant of Swain (See Swain) or as a nickname meaning 'swan'. Swan was of later introduction to Ireland than Swain, being recorded in County Antrim from the mid-17th century.

Sweeney (34) *Scots Gaelic*. This sept was well established in Kintyre, Argyllshire by the year 1200. As one of the most renowned galloglass (mercenary soldier) families they settled in the Fanad peninsula, County Donegal from 1267 and over the subsequent four centuries they fought on the side of the O'Donnells.

Sweeny (1) See Sweeney.

T

Tacey (1) *English*. Derived from the medieval male given name Stace which was a shortened form of Eustace.

Taggart (10) *Scots Gaelic*. Meaning son of the priest the Taggarts or McTaggarts were a sept of Clan Ross. The name became very common in Dumfriesshire. *Irish*. This County Fermanagh sept were hereditary tenants of church lands there.

Tait (2) *English* and *Scottish*. Derived from a nickname meaning 'cheerful' the Taits wre one of the lesser riding clans of the Scottish Borders. In Antrim and Down the name is usually spelt Tate whereas in County Derry Tait predominates.

Tallent (1) *English*. Derived either as an occupational name for a tailor or as a nickname for 'a good swordsman' it was recorded in Counties Carlow and Dublin from the 16th century.

Taphouse (1) *English*. Tap is a common first element in English place names which is derived from an Old English personal name. The name may simply mean Taeppa's house (See House).

Tarr (2) *English*. Recorded as a surname in Bristol it perhaps derived as an occupational name for someone who worked with tar in waterproofing wooden sailing ships.

Tate (3) See Tait.

Taylor (46) *English* and *Scottish.* Derived from the occupational name of tailor. On the English side of the Scottish Borders the Tailors were one of the riding clans. In the Lowlands of Scotland the name was first recorded in the late 13th century while in the Highlands the Taylors or McTaylors were a sept of Clan Cameron in Argyllshire. The name was well known in Ireland from the 14th century but it was the 17th century plantation which established the name in great numbers in Counties Antrim, Down and Derry.

Tedders (1) This English name was recorded in County Mayo as Tethers in the town of Strule in 1857.

Tees (3) *English.* Derived as local names for someone who lived either by a common pasture or by a river or an island.

Teirney (1) See Tierney.

Temple (13) *English.* Derived from one of the houses (known as temples) maintained by the Knights Templar who were a crusading order. In the 30 year period to 1755 no less than 104 foundlings baptised at the Temple Church, London were surnamed Temple or Templar. *Scottish.* Derived from the parish of Temple in Edinburgh which was the principal residence of the Knights Templar in Scotland.

Templeton (1) *Scottish.* Derived from the Ayrshire place name meaning settlement of the Knight's Temple (See Temple) this surname is chiefly found in Ayrshire and Lanarkshire.

Tennis (1) *English.* Meaning son of Tenney, which was derived from the given name Dennis, this name is better known as Tennison or Tennyson (See Dennison).

Thatcher (1) *English.* Derived as an occupational name for a thatcher, i.e. someone who covered roofs with straw (See Slater).

Thelan (1) A variant of Phelan (See Phelan).

Theobald (2) *English.* Derived from the common medieval given name Tebald which in the 17th century was pronounced Tibbald, even when the spelling was Theobald.

Thomas (2) Can be of *English, Scottish* or *Irish* origin. In England and Wales and in Scotland Thomas derived from a very common Anglo-Norman personal name while in Ireland Thomas can be an abbreviation of McThomas or FitzThomas.

Thompson (65) *English* and *Scottish.* Meaning son of Thomas this surname, spelt as Thompson, was the 15th commonest name in England and, as Thomson, was the 5th commonest in Scotland. This distinction in spelling, however, was not perpetuated in Ulster. The Thomsons were one of the lesser riding clans of the Scottish Borders; many of whom settled in County Fermanagh during the 17th century plantation. In the Highlands of Scotland a number of distinct septs of McThomas anglicised their name to Thomson and to McCombe (See McCombe) and Holmes (See Holmes).

Thornton (4) Can be of *English, Scottish* or *Irish* origin. In England and Scotland it derived from a number of place names meaning thorn bush settlement. In the 16th century a family of this name settled in Limerick. In Ireland a number of sept names such as Drennan of Galway, Skehan of Monaghan, Minnagh of Tyrone and Tarrant of Cork were further anglicised to Thornton.

Thorpe (2) *English.* Derived from any number of place names with this Old Norse element meaning hamlet or village.

Tierney (12) *Irish.* There were three septs of this name, with the most important, who were the Lords of Carra, originating in County Mayo. Today Tierney is chiefly associated with Counties Galway, Limerick and Tipperary. A small County Donegal sept of the name will, however, be the origin of most Derry Tierneys.

Tilley (1) *English* and *Scottish.* Derived either from any number of place names in Normandy called Tilly or from the occupational name for a husbandman.

Timmins (1) *English.* Meaning son of little Timm this surname is derived from some unrecorded Old English personal name. Timothy was not in use in England until Tudor times so it is unlikely that Timm derived from it. In Ireland a sept called Timmons, who were a branch of the Barretts, established themselves in County Mayo.

Timoney (1) *Irish.* This sept originated in South Donegal and through time the name spread into the adjoining parts of Tyrone, Fermanagh and Leitrim.

Tinneny (1) *Irish.* Found chiefly in Cavan and Leitrim this surname is thought to be a variant of the County Down sept name of Timpany.

Tinney (3) A County Tyrone sept whose name originally meant son of the fox. It was further anglicised to Fox (See Fox).

Tipler (1) *English.* Derived from the occupational name for a seller of ale, called a tapster.

Toal (1) *Irish.* This County Monaghan sept is distinct from O'Toole (See O'Toole) although their names in gaelic were indentical.

Todd (3) *English* and *Scottish.* Derived from a Northern English nickname for someone thought to resemble a fox, for example in cunning or in having red hair. The surname was first recorded in Scotland in the late 13th century. In addition the Todds were septs of Clans Gordon and MacTavish.

Toland (27) *Irish.* Originating in South Donegal many members of this sept migrated to Mayo with some of the leading O'Donnells in 1602. In Mayo they became better known as Tolan.

Toner (3) *Irish.* Tracing their descent from Eoghan, son of the 5th century Niall of the Nine Hostages this sept, which originated on the west bank of the Foyle near Lifford, County Donegal, later migrated to Counties Derry and Armagh. The name also originated in England where it derived as a local name for someone who lived on a farm.

Tonner (1) A variant of Toner. (See Toner).

Tope (2) *English.* Also recorded as Toop and Toope this name derived from the Old Norse personal name Topi. Tope was recorded as a surname in the Domesday Book of 1086.

Torney (1) *Irish.* A variant found chiefly in Fermanagh of the sept name of Dorney which originated in County Cork and North Kerry.

Torrens (5) *Scottish.* Derived from the place names of Torrance in Stirlingshire and Lanarkshire. Robert Torrens, a noted advocate of assisted emigration to Australia in the 1830s, was descended from a family who settled in County Derry in the 18th century. River Torrens on which Adelaide stands was named after him.

Tosh (3) A shortened form of Mackintosh (See McIntosh).

Totton (2) *English.* Totten and Totton are common names throughout Northern Ireland. They perhaps derive from the Nottinghamshire place name of Toton meaning Tofi's settlement. Tofi was an Old Norse personal name.

Tourish (1) *Irish.* This is a variant of the County Tyrone sept name of Horish which was also anglicised to Caldwell (See Caldwell), Houriskey, Waters (See Watters) and Tidings.

Townsend (1) *English.* Derived from a local name for someone who lived at the extremity of a village it was recorded in Cork from the mid-17th century.

Toye (4) *English.* Derived as a nickname for 'a light-hearted person'. *Irish.* A variant of the County Roscommon sept name of Towey. It may also be a variant of the County Galway sept name of Tuohy.

Tracey (23) *Irish.* There were at one time three distinct septs of this name; in Galway they were a branch of the O'Maddens; in Cork they were of the same stock as the O'Donovans and in Leix the Traceys were Lords of Slievemargy.

Tracy (1) See Tracey.

Traill (1) *Scottish.* Derived from an unidentified place name in Northern Scotland this name was recorded in Aberdeen and in Fifeshire in the 14th century.

Trainor (4) *Irish.* Meaning son of the strong man, and also anglicised as McTreanor and McCrainor, this name is chiefly found in Counties Armagh, Monaghan and Tyrone. Trainor was also known in England from the 13th century where it derived as an occupational name for a trapper.

Travers (5) *English.* Derived either as a local name for someone who lived by a bridge or ford or as an occupational name for a toll collector. *Irish.* The County Leitrim sept name of Trower was anglicised to Travers.

Trayherne (1) In all of Ireland the only reference to Trayherne in the telephone directories in in Derry.

Traynor (1) See Trainor.

Treacher (1) *English.* Derived as a nickname for 'a devious person'.

Trotter (4) *English* and *Scottish.* Derived as an occupational name for a messenger the Trotters of Berwickshire were one of the riding clans of the Scottish Borders. The name was also common in Durham.

Tuck (1) *English.* A recorded variant of Tooke which was derived from the Old Norse personal name Toki.

Tucker (3) *English*. In Southwest England, especially in Devon, Tucker derived as an occupational name for a fuller (See Walker).

Turner (9) *English* and *Scottish*. Derived as an occupational name for a lathe-worker. In Scotland Turner was a common name in Aberdeenshire and Kirkcudbrightshire. In addition they were one of the lesser riding clans of the Scottish Borders while in the Highlands the Turners were a sept of Clan Lamont.

Turton (1) *English*. Derived from the Lancashire place name meaning Thor's settement. Thor was a common first element in Scandinavian personal names. This name is now as common in the Midlands as it is in Lancashire and Yorkshire.

Tweed (1) *English* and *Scottish*. Derived from a local name for someone living on the banks of the River Tweed which flows between Northeast England and Southeast Scotland.

Twells (2) *English*. A recorded variant of Attwell which derived as a local name for someone who lived by a spring or stream.

U

Ussher (1) *English* and *Scottish*. Derived as an occupational name for a gate-keeper it was originally the Usher's job to keep the door of the King's apartment. By tradition the Usshers in Ireland descend from a member of the Neville family, who was Usher to King John when he came to Ireland in 1210.

V

Vail (1) *English*. Derived as an occupational name for a watchman. *Scottish*. A shortened form of McVail which in turn was a variant of McPhail or McFaul, meaning son of Paul. (See McFaul).

Vallelly (1) *Irish*. Recorded in 17th century records in Armagh and Monaghan as McIlvallelly this County Armagh sept name is now known as Vallelly.

Vance (3) *English*. This variant of Fenn derived as a local name for someone who lived in a low-lying, marshy area.

Vaughan (3) *Welsh.* Derived as an epithet, from Welsh Bychan (meaning little), to distinguish between father and son who had the same name. This common Welsh name has been recorded in Ireland from the early 16th century. *Irish.* Two distinct septs, one located in South Galway and the other in County Sligo, of Mohan or Mahon usually anglicised their name to Vaughan when they spread into Munster. Mahon, therefore, is usually quite distinct from McMahon. (See McMahon).

Vernor (1) *Scottish.* Derived either as a variant of the Germanic personal name Warner or from the Midlothian place name of Vernours. It was recorded as a surname in Edinburgh from the early 15th century.

Verrall (1) Only recorded in Derry in the Northern Ireland phone book. It may be a variant of the County Longford sept name of Farrell or Ferrall (See Farrell).

Vickery (2) *English.* Derived as an occupational name for a parish priest it was introduced to County Cork in the mid-17th century.

Vig (2) Originating from the small town of Kartarpur, in the upper reaches of the tributaries of the Indus, in the State of Punjab in Northern India this name, meaning warriors, came to Derry from New Delhi in 1954. The original bearer of this name in Derry first lived with his relatives the Chadas (See Chada).

Vij (3) Originating from the State of Punjab in Northern India this name came to Derry in the 1930s.

Villa (10) This name is very much concentrated in the Derry area yet it is unrecorded anywhere in County Derry in 1831. This surname, however, is found in both Italy and Spain where it derived as a local name for someone who lived in a village.

Vine (1) *English.* Derived either as a local name for someone who lived near a vineyard or as an occupational name for a vine dresser. In the Middle Ages vine growing was common in Southern England and Vine is an old surname in Dorset and Sussex. The surname was recorded in Aberdeen, Scotland in the early 16th century.

W

Wade (7) In addition to being a corruption of McQuaid (See McQuaid) Wade can be an English name derived either from an Old English personal name or from a local name for someone who lived by a ford.

Walden (1) *English.* Derived from place names in Essex, Hertfordshire and North Yorkshire meaning the valley of the Britons. It is believed that Walden originally referred to enclaves of Welsh-speaking people noted by the Anglo-Saxons.

Walker (47) *English* and *Scottish.* In the North and West of England Walker derived as an occupational name for a fuller (see Tucker). In the Middle Ages it was the fuller's job to scour and thicken raw cloth by "walking" or trampling upon it in a trough filled with water. Walker also became widespread in Scotland where it was first recorded in the early 14th century. In Ireland the name is most common in Counties Arntrim, Down and Derry.

Wallace (22) *English* and *Scottish.* Meaning Welshman or Celt this term was applied by the conquering Normans to the native population of England and Wales. In Scotland Wallace derived as a native name for a Strathclyde Briton. It first appeared in the 12th century in Ayrshire and Renfrewshire which were parts of the ancient Celtic Kingdom of Strathclyde. As Clan Wallace they acquired extensive lands in Ayrshire.

Walls (1) *English* and *Scottish.* Derived from local names for someone who lived either by a stone wall or by a spring or stream. In Scotland the name also derived as a variant of Wallace (See Wallace). In Ireland Walls will be a distinct name from Wall. The surname Wall can be traced to Anglo-Norman families named de Vale (which derived as a local name in Southern England for someone who lived in a valley) who settled in the area between Limerick and Waterford in the 13th century.

Walmsley (1) *English.* Derived from the Lancashire place name of Walmersley meaning lake by the wood.

Walsh (23) *Irish.* Meaning Welshman this name, the fourth most numerous in Ireland, was given to many of the soldier-adventurers who followed in the wake of the Anglo-Norman invasion of the late 12th century. As the name arose independently all over Ireland the Walshes didn't develop along sept lines. Walsh was gaelicised to "Breathnach" which in turn was anglicised to Brannagh and Brannick.

Ward (40) In England this name derived as an occupational name for a watchman or guard. Most Wards in Ireland, however, are of Gaelic Irish origin. Meaning son of the bard, and also anglicised as McAward and McWard, septs of this name were hereditary poets to both the O'Kellys of Galway and to the O'Donnells of Donegal. The Wards of Donegal were based at Lettermacaward near Glenties. In Scotland McWard generally became Baird (see Baird) but not Ward.

Wardlow (1) *Scottish.* Derived from a number of minor place names called Wardlaw meaning watch hill it was recorded as a surname in the Scottish Borders in the early 14th century.

Warke (5) *English* and *Scottish.* Derived from the Northumberland place name of Wark on the River Tweed meaning fort. It has been recorded in Counties Derry and Donegal since the mid-17th century.

Warnock (5) *Scots Gaelic.* A shortened form of the Argyllshire sept name MacIlvernock, meaning son of the servant of Ernan, which is found mainly in Lanarkshire. *Irish.* The County Down sept of McGillavearnoge, meaning son of the devotee of Mearnog, was anglicised to Warnock.

Warren (3) Can be of *English, Scottish* or *Irish* origin. Derived from the French name of Varenne Anglo-Norman families of this name acquired vast estates in Counties Meath, Kildare and Offaly. In Scotland Warren was recorded as a surname from the early 13th century and in Ireland the County Kerry sept name of Murnane was anglicised to Warren.

Warrick (1) *English* and *Scottish.* This variant of Warwick was derived from the county town of Warwickshire meaning outlying settlement. In Scotland the name was chiefly found in Dumfriesshire and Kirkcudbrightshire.

Wasson (4) *English* and *Scottish.* Derived from the Norman personal name Wazo. In Scotland it may also be a variant of Watson (See Watson).

Waterkamp (2) *German.* The grandfather of the bearer of the name was born in Germany where the name was pronounced Vaterkamp. The first element Water derived as a local name for someone who lived by a stretch of water while Kamp derived as a local name for someone who lived in the countryside. The Great-Grandfather of the Derry Waterkamps may have been born in the German-speaking portion of Poland.

Waterstone (2) *Scottish.* Originally Waterstoun, meaning Walter's place, this name derived from three places of that name in Angus, Midlothian and Renfrewshire. The surname was also recorded as Waterson.

Watkins (2) Meaning son of young Walter (See Watson) this form of the name was most common in Wales and adjacent English counties and in Devon.

Watson (21) *English* and *Scottish.* Meaning son of Watt, which in turn was derived from the Old German name Walter, this name became most numerous in Aberdeenshire and Banffshire. In the Highlands of Scotland Watt, McWatt and Watson have become confused as the Watt septs attached to Clans Forbes and Buchanan also anglicised their name to Watson.

Watt (3) See Watson.

Watters (3) Can be of *English, Scottish* or *Irish* origin. In England and Scotland Watters was derived from the personal name Walter (See Watson). In the Highlands of Scotland the Caithness name of McWatters was made Watters. Several Irish names such as Hiskey, Whoriskey and Toorish were anglicised to Waters.

Watts (5) Meaning son of Watt (See Watson) this form of the name was most common in Southern England especially in Gloucestershire, Somersetshire and Wiltshire.

Weaver (1) *English* and *Scottish.* Derived either as an occuptional name for a weaver or from the River Weaver in Cheshire meaning winding streams. In some cases Scots Gaelic McNider, meaning son of the weaver, was anglicised to Weaver.

Webb (6) *English.* Derived from the occupational name for a weaver this name has been established in Ireland since the mid-17th century.

Webdale (1) *English.* Derived from a now unidentified place name of Websdale. Dale, meaning valley, is a common element in English place names.

Webster (2) *English* and *Scottish.* Derived from the occupational name for a weaver it is chiefly found in Yorkshire, Lancashire and the Midlands. Webster was recorded in Scotland from the early 15th century and in Ireland from the mid-17th century.

Weir (3) Can be of *English, Scottish* or *Irish* origin. In England it derived as a local name for someone who lived by a dam. The name was recorded in Scotland from the 12th century. In addition the Scots Gaelic name of McNair was anglicised to Weir. In Ireland, the County Armagh septs of McMoyer and of McGillaweer were anglicised to Weir.

Welch (4) A variant of Walsh. See Walsh.

Wells (3) *English* and *Scottish.* Derived from a local name for someone who lived near a spring or stream it was recorded as a surname in both Scotland and Ireland from the 13th century.

West (2) *English* and *Scottish.* Derived either as a local name for someone who lived to the west of a settlement or as a regional name for someone who had migrated from further west it was recorded in Scotland as a surname in Perthshire and West Lothian.

Whelan (2) A variant of Phelan. See Phelan.

White (30) Can be of *English, Scottish* or *Irish* origin. In England and the Lowlands of Scotland this name derived as a nickname for someone with 'fair hair' or 'fair complexion'. In the Scottish Highlands White was one of the colour names adopted by members of Clans MacGregor and Lamont on their proscription in the 17th century. In Ireland those names which contained the gaelic epithet ban or gael, meaning white, such as Bane, Bawn, Kilbane and Galligan were frequently anglicised to White.

Whiteman (2) *English.* Derived either from the Old English name Hwitmann or from an occupational name for a servant to a person called White (See White) this name was largely confined to Huntingdonshire and Shropshire.

Whiteside (5) *English* and *Scottish.* Derived from a number of minor place names meaning white slope. Whiteside was recorded as both Quhyteside and Whytsyid in Lanarkshire, Scotland in the 17th century.

Whitsitt (1) Family tradition in this case claims Whitsitt is a corruption of Whiteside (See Whiteside) which arose from a late 19th century mistake by an elderly doctor in County Monaghan who wrongly registered the birth of a male child as Whitsitt as opposed to Whiteside.

Whittaker (1) *English.* Derived from a number of place names meaning either white field or wheat field. This surname is largely confined to the North of England.

Whitters (1) *English.* Derived as a local name for someone who lived in a white house. By comparison the Lancashire name of Whitter was derived from the occupational name for a bleacher or a whitewasher.

Whittingham (1) *English* and *Scottish.* Derived from place names in Lancashire and Northumberland and from the lands of Whittinghame in East Lothian, meaning the homestead of Hwita's people.

Whoriskey (12) *Irish.* Recorded in County Roscommon in 1591 as O'Fworishe this sept name was anglicised in Donegal to Whoriskey in the first instance and then to Waters and Watters (See Watters).

Whyte (3) See White,

Wilkes (1) *English.* A contracted form of the Old English name Willock which meant little William (See Williams).

Wilkinson (4) *English* and *Scottish.* Meaning son of young William the Wilkinsons were one of the lesser riding clans on the English side of the Scottish Borders. In the Highlands of Scotland McQuilken was anglicised to Wilkinson (See McQuilkin).

Williams (17) *English* and *Scottish.* Meaning son of William it was derived from the Old German personal name William which was introduced to Britain by the Normans. Williams became an extremely common surname in England and Wales whereas in Scotland Williamson, as opposed to Williams, was more favoured.

Furthermore the Highlands name of McWilliams (See McWilliams) was anglicised to Williamson.

Williamson (8) See Williams.

Willis (6) *English* and *Scottish.* Meaning son of William (See Williams) this name is common in Counties Antrim and Down.

Willman (2) *English.* Derived as an occupational name for a servant to a person called William (See Williams).

Willsher (1) *English.* Derived from the county name of Wiltshire.

Wilson (6) *English* and *Scottish.* This is another name which is derived from the personal name William (See Williams). It is estimated that 80% of Ulster Wilsons are of Scottish descent; Wilson was a common name throughout the Lowlands of Scotland. Furthermore the Wilsons were septs of Clan Gunn in Caithness and Sutherland and of Clan Innes in Banffshire.

Wilton (3) *English.* Derived from a number of place names with different meanings, depending on their location, such as settlement among the willows in the North and East of England and settlement by a spring or well in the Southwest.

Wing (1) *English.* Derived from place names in Buckinghamshire and Rutland meaning Weohthun's people and field respectively.

Winnard (1) *English.* This variant of Winyard, which is found in Lancashire, derived either as a local name for someone who lived by a vineyard or as an occupational name for someone who worked in one (See Vine).

Winston (1) *English.* Derived either from an Old English personal name or from a number of place names called Winston and Winstone. A family of this name settled in Waterford in 1573.

Wiseman (1) *English* and *Scottish.* Derived from a nickname for 'a wise or learned man'. Wiseman is an old surname in Angus and Moray, Scotland and it has been recorded in County Cork since the 16th century.

Wishart (1) *Scottish.* Derived from the Norman personal name Wischard this surname appears frequently in Scottish records from the year 1200 onwards.

Wisner (1) Recorded also as Wisener and Wysner this name is very much located in the Coleraine/North Antrim area. The bearer of the name in Derry came here from Coleraine in the early 1980s. Family tradition claims the name is German in origin. It is probably derived from a nickname for 'a wise or learned person'.

Withington (1) *English.* Derived from a number of place names meaning willow settlement.

Wolsely (1) *English.* Derived from the Staffordshire place name of Wolseley meaning Wulfsige's wood.

Wong (1) There are 16 references to this Chinese surname in the telephone directory of Northern Ireland and all but one of them (i.e. in Derry) are living in the east of the Province.

Wood (3) Can be of *English, Scottish* or *Irish* origin. In England and Scotland Wood, a common surname in both countries, derived as a local name for someone who lived in or near a wood. Woods, however, is a rather uncommon name in Britain. By contrast, in Ireland, Woods is ten times more numerous than Wood and most will be of Gaelic Irish stock. A number of sept names such as McEnhill and McElhone of Tyrone, Coyle and McIlhoyle (See Coyle) of Donegal and Kielty of Down were anglicised to Woods. Wood and Woods are, therefore, two distinct names although the passage of time will have blurred this distinction.

Wooding (1) *English.* Derived as a local name for someone who lived at a place where wood had been cut.

Woods (7) See Wood.

Wooster (1) *English.* Derived from the city of Worcester meaning the Roman fort of the tribe called Wigoran.

Wray (19) *English.* This name is especially associated with Yorkshire where it derived from a number of minor place names in Northern England meaning nook or remote place. In the 16th century a Yorkshire family named Wray did settle in the Derry area. Not only has Wray become confused with Rea (see Rea) it has, in some instances, become Rowe (See Row).

Wright (15) Can be of *English, Scottish* or *Irish* origin. In Northern England and the Lowlands of Scotland Wright derived as an occupational name for a carpenter or joiner. In the Highlands of Scotland the Wrights were a sept of Clan McIntryre while in Ireland McAteer (See McAteer) was anglicised to Wright.

Wtson (1) This is a misspelling of Watson by British Telecom. (See Watson).

Wylie (24) *English*. Derived from a number of different place names such as Willey meaning willow wood or River Wiley meaning tricky river i.e. a river liable to flood. *Scottish*. In Ulster Wylie is more likely to be of Scottish origin. Wylie is a common name in Scotland where it was derived from the personal name William (See William). It was recorded in Dumfriesshire in the late 14th century.

Y

Yates (1) *English* and *Scottish*. Derived either as a local name for someone who lived near a gate or as an occupational name for a gate-keeper. A family of this name settled in Dublin in the 17th century. The County Sligo literary and artistic family of Yeats trace their descent from Jervis Yeats of Dublin who died in 1712.

Young (32) *English* and *Scottish*. Derived as a nickname to distinguish father and son with the same christian name. In England this name was most numerous in County Durham and in the South West of the country. The Youngs of Culdaff, County Donegal originated from Devon. The Youngs were one of the lesser riding clans of the Scottish Borders. In Ireland the gaelic epithet Og, meaning young, which frequently accompanied Irish forenames sometimes gave rise to the surname Young.

Younge (1) See Young.

Z

Zammit (1) Originating from Valletta in Malta this name arrived in Derry in the 1880s. The original bearer of the name arrived in Derry as chief engineer on the S.S. Harrington.